Heagle,John
On The Way.

On
the
WAY

On
the
WAY

by
John Heagle

Photographs by
Todd Brennan

THE THOMAS MORE PRESS
Chicago, Illinois

Grateful acknowledgment to the following for permission to reprint:

Lines from "The Sound of Trees" from *The Poetry of Robert Frost*, edited by Edward Connery Lathem. © 1916, 1969, by Holt, Rinehart and Winston, 383 Madison Ave., New York, N.Y. 10017.

Lines from "But God's Own Descent" © 1944, 1956, 1962 by Robert Frost. Reprinted by permission by Holt, Rinehart and Winston Publishers.

Excerpts from THE JERUSALEM BIBLE, copyright © 1966 by Darton, Longman & Todd, Ltd. and Doubleday & Company, Inc. Used by permission of the publisher.

Excerpts from *The Seven Storey Mountain* and *The Sign of Jonas* by Thomas Merton. Copyright © by Thomas Merton 1948 and 1956. Reprinted by permission of the publisher, Harcourt, Brace, Jovanovich, Inc.

Excerpt from J. B. by Archibald MacLeish. Copyright © 1956, 1957, 1958 by Archibald MacLeish. Reprinted by permission of the publisher, Houghton, Mifflin Co.

Portions of the material in this book first appeared in the newsletter *You.*

ISBN 0-88347-132-9

Contents

For Fran

Introduction

CENTURIES ago a Hebrew poet looked at his life and his world and tried to make sense out of what he saw. Like poets in every age, he struggled to find meaning in the joys and sorrows, the dreams and disappointments of the human journey. What he gives us in the Book of Proverbs is not a theoretical world of ideas and principles, but a practical way of seeking wisdom. He was not concerned about solving the scientific riddles of the universe or with explaining the philosophical origins of thought. He was interested in living— daily living. His theoretical conclusions were at best tentative. But the poet was sure of something. He was convinced that there must be a vision by which we walk, an energy by which we live, for "without a vision, the people perish" (Pv 11:14).

As we move toward the 3rd millennium of the Christian era, the need for such a vision appears all the more urgent. The voices around us are confused and disparate. Human values are in conflict. We find ourselves searching for a vision upon which we can stake our lives.

I am not speaking here of a theory or of an abstract set of principles. I am not referring to a set of moral directives or a collection of doctrinal statements about human life. I am speaking of a *way of living*—a sustaining power by which we grow toward life. The issue that concerns Christians today is the same one that haunted the Hebrew poets of old. It is not so much a question of what we can know, but of what we are to *do*. Even more basically, it is a question of who we are to *become* and how we are to *live*.

What is the vision that can shape our future? What is the creative energy that will permeate our daily lives? Where is the insight into our experience which is so powerful that it will transform our way of understanding and living?

These are not new questions. They are as old as the Hebrew poets, as ancient as the prophets, as perduring as the seasons. They have stirred in every age and in every heart. They have been asked in different words and in different circumstances. They have been raised in different times and places. But in the end they are the same question, the same underlying quest for human meaning. In some mysterious way all the questions seem to converge in one question—the one which Thomas asked Jesus on the night of their last Passover: "Lord, we do not know where you are going; how can we know the way?"

How can we know the way? Thomas' question may be old, but it must be asked anew in every generation. Out of the ferment of every age the spirit stirs and the heart seeks. Today it is our own voices that we hear asking: How are *we* to know the way—we who live with a world in turmoil and a church in transition? How are we to recognize the vision and claim the energy of life?

The answer is the same for us as it was for Thomas and for Christians of all ages: "I AM THE WAY..."

It is significant that Jesus did not respond in the language of theological speculation. He did not say that he would tell us the answer or that he would explain the vision. He simply pointed to himself. The response to our most basic questions about life comes from a person, because the answer *is* a person—the person of Jesus. Do not look for a theory or an explanation, Jesus seems to be telling us, just come to know me. I am the way. I am the vision become flesh. I am the journey, the passing over to freedom, the unfolding of life, the breakthrough to truth. I am the Word behind all words, the wayfarer in the heart of every pilgrim.

This is not a new revelation. As Christians we know and believe that Jesus is the answer to human life. We trust that his journey is redemptive. The renewal has enabled us to understand more clearly how central the paschal mystery is in our faith. Today our catechesis better reflects this focus and our liturgy more effectively celebrates it.

But this is not enough. Just as the ancient questions of meaning—the questions of the Hebrew poets, the prophets, and Thomas—must be asked anew in each person's life and in every age, so too must the answer be heard again in each person's life and in each new age.

In the past several years I have discovered the question of Thomas recurring in my life as though it were a new question. I have also heard the response of Jesus with new clarity and urgency. I hear the question; I trust the response. But how can I live out the answer more authentically? How does the Lord's Way become my way? How can I become a Christian disciple in today's world?

This book is an attempt to answer these questions out of my personal experience, reflection, and prayer. To do so, I have returned not only to the ancient biblical questions and responses, but also to the earliest name for Christians. In scripture a name is more than a label. It is an expression of identity and mission. A name conveys the reality and meaning of the person who bears it. The earliest name given to the disciples of Jesus was not "Christians" but "Followers of the Way." This name indicates the essential manner in which Christians are called to live out the vision of Jesus—by following and sharing in his journey toward life.

In the meditations which follow I will explore what it means to follow the Way of Jesus in our daily lives. Each of the chapters focuses on an aspect of the paschal journey. These "passages" are not intended to be viewed as isolated experiences in our lives. They are not so much chronological stages through which we pass as they are dimensions of daily life. They are journeys of the heart. Their sequence in this book does not necessarily reflect their sequence in our lives. At times some of these experiences of "passing over" may occur simultaneously. There may be a part of us that is running away or wandering, while another dimension of our lives is setting out, breaking through, or coming home.

What matters most is that we see the Lord's pattern reflected in our own. With Paul we can say that "we die daily," and we might add that we also rise daily. Easter is a moveable feast—an experience that moves through us and in us to transform our lives after the pattern of Jesus.

It is my hope that these meditations will enable other Christians to understand the passover process as it unfolds in their lives. The vision we see is the life we share—a life which, however ordinary or commonplace, marks us out as Followers of the Way.

CHAPTER ONE

Jesus: Forerunner of Humanity

"We have this as a sure and steadfast anchor of the soul, a hope that enters into the inner shrine behind the curtain, where Jesus has gone as a forerunner on our behalf..."

—Hebrews 6:19–20 (RSV)

WHEN the monk Paulinus first brought the gospel of Christianity to Northumbria his message caused a lively debate among the people. After much discussion King Edwin convoked a special meeting of his counselors to decide whether or not they would accept this new way of life. The meeting took place on a winter's night in one of the great halls of the castle. As the noblemen assembled, a blazing fire lit up their faces and cast shadows across the room. The heat from the fireplace was barely enough to take the chill out of the air, for at either end of the hall a doorway stood open to the night.

As the evening wore on, one of the counselors was distracted by a solitary sparrow which flew into the room through the doorway at the far end of the hall. At first the small bird was dazed by the light of the fire and the shadows that played across the ceiling. For a few moments it fluttered

silently about the room, unsure of its direction and confused by the new surroundings. Then, as suddenly as it had appeared, the sparrow flew out the other doorway and disappeared into the night.

For a few minutes the counselor stared into the darkness. Then he looked reflectively at the fire. His eyes became quiet and pensive. When it was his turn to speak, he turned to the other members of the group and said: "Our lives are like the flight of the sparrow which fluttered for a moment in this hall. At birth we come out of an unknown darkness. For a few moments we move through the warmth and the flickering shadows of life. We are baffled by our surroundings and fascinated by the movements we see and the sounds we hear. We seek for understanding. We draw near to the light and the source of warmth. We have glimpses of truth and moments of joy, but, in the end, it all slips away. As suddenly as we appeared, we are gone. We return to the night and we are forgotten."

The counselor paused for a moment and studied the faces of his colleagues. His next words were spoken slowly and with deliberation: "Whence have we come? Where are we going? Is there any meaning in the words and gestures and the fleeting moments of our lives? If Christianity can tell us something about the night from which we've come or the darkness toward which we are going, it would be well worth our hearing."

An Ancient Parable, A Contemporary Quest

The story of the sparrow and its flight has more than historical interest. It is not just an attractive legend out of Christianity's past. It is a parable for our time. It is a description of the search for an authentic spirituality. The sparrow is a symbol of modern selfhood. It represents the confused but persistent search for personal significance.

More important than the sparrow, however, is the figure of the king's counselor. He is a man of wisdom and insight. The questions which he asks are as ancient as the hunger of the heart for God. They are as contemporary as our quest to find meaning in a confused world.

The setting of this story is distant from our experience, but we recognize the issues which it raises. We too are interested in the direction and meaning of the human journey. With the help of the behavioral sciences we have studied the stages of psychic growth. We have explored the unconscious and debated its contents. We have developed new forms and approaches to therapy. Through developmental psychology we have mapped out the turning points and the breakthroughs of the psyche.

Despite the popular interest in psychology, however, the journey of life is still a bewildering and dark mystery. It is a fluttering in the night, a search for light and warmth, a quest to understand.

Like Edwin's counselor we are also concerned about the origin and destiny of our lives. For the most part our interest has taken a practical, scientific bent. Through genetics and the technology related to birth control we have gained a new understanding of the structure of life. In the research surrounding test tube babies and the possibility of cloning we have even taken some steps toward controlling the reproductive process. The same is true of the other doorway that opens into the night—death and the afterlife.

But these are only glimpses. They do not touch the real mystery of life or of death. The deeper issues transcend the historical circumstances that surround us. They cannot be grasped by the tools of science, for they are questions of the heart and issues of the soul. They are the same questions which were raised that winter night in England: Where have I come from? Where am I going? What is the dark mystery that defines the boundaries of my life? Are the questions and the seeking, the struggling and the waiting, the doubts and the decisions only a fluttering about, a brief and futile search for light before the darkness envelops me?

Today our experience echoes the conviction of King Edwin's counselor: If Christianity can tell us something about the night from which we've come or the darkness toward which we are going, it would be well worth our hearing. If the gospel can speak of the brief journey of human life with meaning and hope, it would be good news indeed.

Refocusing Our Vision

Renewal is another word for rediscovering the essential in our tradition. It is a reshaping of our inward vision, an attempt to reformulate the central meaning of our faith in words and rites that celebrate the age-old questions in contemporary form. Renewal is also a refocusing—a movement away from the periphery toward the center, away from the nonessential toward the essential. It demands a radical change of heart and a willingness to change the way in which we understand ourselves and God.

For the past several years this task of rediscovery and refocusing has been the primary concern of the church. In an effort to return to the normative experience of the gospel, we have put aside some of the cultural accretions that accumulated over the centuries. We have learned again that Christianity is more than a doctrine, more than an explanation of life, more than a set of moral guidelines or an established mode of worship.

Christianity is a way of living. That is its secret—it is a way, a journey, a process of life that is rooted in the transforming journey of Christ through death to new life.

The center of Christian faith is Christ. This is a truism, but it is a reality that needs to be asserted again and again. "In times past," writes the author of Hebrews, "God spoke to our fathers through the prophets; in the final age, he has spoken to us through his Son, whom he has made heir of all things and through whom he first created the universe" (He 1:1-2).

Our ability to find a way to God is dependent on Jesus who became the Lord of life. Jesus did not discover a scientific secret to explain the dark mystery of life. He did not develop a new political system or propose a revolutionary social theory.

He gave us no medical answer for disease. He did not take away human suffering.

Jesus: the Way

Why is Jesus so important then? Why is he so central to all that we believe and do? The traditional answer to this question is that Jesus is our savior. Through his sufferings we are redeemed. But what do these words mean? How do they touch our lives? What did Jesus discover about human experience?

Jesus discovered that at the heart of life, in the midst of its pain and struggle, its doubt and uncertainty, there is the reality of unconditional love. That reality is not a cosmic force or an abstract truth, but a loving presence. Jesus refers to this inbreaking of love into life as the kingdom of God. He speaks of God as Abba—dearest Father. It is a name of profound intimacy and endearment.

When Jesus gathered his friends together to celebrate the Passover for the last time, he told them about his union with the Father and his desire that all of his followers share this unity. He summarized the meaning of his life in these simple words:

> *I came from the Father and have come*
> *into the world*
> *and now I leave the world to go to the*
> *Father (Jn 16:28).*

These are significant words. In them Jesus describes his life as a journey which originates with the Father and ultimately finds its fulfillment in his eternal presence. Jesus invites us to view life with his eyes. He challenges us to make his journey our own. He reveals the promise that lies hidden in the "dreamcrossed twilight between birth and dying" (T. S. Eliot).

The origin of life is not a cosmic night. Our destiny is not oblivion. We come from creative love and move toward the eternal warmth of light. We find our origin and our destiny in God. We can echo the Lord's own words: We have come from the Father and have come into the world, and now we leave the world to go to the Father.

No longer is the human journey an aimless wandering or a confused groping in the shadows. It is a true adventure—a coming toward light and truth, a movement with form and direction. The pain and the struggle become integrated into a life-giving process.

The existence of Jesus in the world gives a sacred quality to all of life. In him our journey finds a direction. It becomes, in the words of Romano Guardini, "a coming and a returning. It is a passing through, which forges through the deepest abyss of life and bears everything up into the holy beginning of the redemption and the new creation."

Becoming Contemporary with Christ

"Jesus lived a long time ago. I believe he was a good man and that he understood the meaning of life. I admire him and I accept the basic truths that he taught. But I don't consider myself to be his follower. How do you follow a figure out of the past?''

These words were spoken by a young college student several years ago. They reflect an honesty and forthrightness that I respect. They also reveal an attitude that is widespread among those who claim that they are followers of Christ. Many people think of the Christian life as following the teachings of a distant historical figure. They would agree with everything the college student said except for his conclusion. They would not understand why he could believe in the teachings of Jesus and not be his disciple.

Perhaps this young man's reasoning is more consistent than it first appears. Too often it is the Christ out of the past rather than the Lord of the present that we follow. This is not a living Christ who can touch our lives now, but a sacred figure from the pages of history. In one sense the college student is simply echoing the words of St. Paul: "If Christ was not raised to life, then your faith is worthless"(1 Co 15:17).

How can the gospel become a living Word? How does the mystery of Christ touch our lives and transform our hearts? Even if Jesus discovered the way to life, it is empty and useless unless it becomes a living encounter with God in the present.

How does the experience of Jesus become ours? This is the same question that Soren Kierkegaard was asking when he wrote: "How do we become contemporary with Christ?" How do we enter into communion with his consciousness and his commitment?

To become contemporary with Christ is to encounter the Lord in the struggle and choices of our present experience. Paul became contemporary with Christ on the road to Damascus; Stephen in his willingness to suffer; the martyrs in their dying; the mystics in their encounter with the Father through the prayer of Jesus.

To become contemporary with Christ is to open ourselves to the risen Lord who is present in our lives. This is not an act of pretending. It does not mean that we enter a make-believe world where Jesus still walks the earth as he once did the roads of Judea. Nor does it imply that we project ourselves backwards in time.

To become contemporary with Christ is to come alive to the Lord in the present experience of our personal journey. It is to recognize that the church is the Body of Christ, the extension of the risen savior in time and space. Jesus of Nazareth has become Christ the Lord. He is the head of his body, the church. It is the whole Christ, encountered in faith and lived in love, with whom we become contemporaneous.

As baptized Christians we participate in the dying and rising of Christ through the sacramental life of the church. The recent liturgical reforms and the renewed rites of the sacraments have refocused the church's awareness of the central experience of salvation. In the documents of the Second Vatican Council and in the decrees of implementation which followed, there is an under-lying theme. That theme is the centrality of the paschal mystery as the basis of Christian spiritu-ality.

The paschal mystery is more than the saving journey which Jesus made through his life, death, and resurrection. The paschal mystery is the jour-ney which Christ continues to make in the dying and rising of the members of his body. It is the pattern of transformation which is traced out in the life of every Christian who has been initiated into the pilgrim community.

In his letters to the early Christian communi-ties, St. Paul outlines this mystery of salvation. He sees Christian life as a dying with Christ, a ris-ing with Christ, and a living in Christ. The phrases, with Christ and in Christ, are some of the most frequently used words in Paul's writings. They express his mystical sense that Christians reproduce the paschal journey of Christ in their own flesh. "Christ died for us," writes Louis Bouyer, "not in order to dispense us from dying, but rather to make us capable of dying with mean-ing, of dying to the life of the old man, in order to live again as the new man who will die no more."

The Paschal Character of Every Day

The sacraments are celebrations in community of our encounter with the Lord and our personal sharing in his pasch. But what of daily life? What of the inward moments that are not directly re-lated to sacramental celebrations? How do they find their meaning? How are they sealed with the

Spirit? How can we see the presence of the Lord's cross and victory in the events of daily living?

Let us be more specific. The major turning points of our lives are ritualized communal celebrations—a birthday party, an anniversary dinner, a graduation luncheon, a wedding banquet, a funeral wake. These are moments when our families and friends gather to mark the passage of time and to affirm the transition to a new stage of life.

The same is true of sacramental life. Each of the sacraments is a communal celebration of life in transition. In this case it is the inward growth of the Spirit that we affirm and celebrate in festive gathering. But what of the in-between moments? What of those times in our lives that are neither peak experiences nor turning points, but simply the unfolding of life? How do we find a way of celebrating the ordinary? What meaning can we find in the daily demands and the struggles of the Christian passover?

Our greatest deeds are our inward decisions for life. The deepest meaning of our lives remains hidden to everyone except ourselves and God. The most significant turning points in our journey are often realized without fanfare and even without words. But these are sacred moments all the same. They are rooted in the mystery of Christ. They are an integral part of our passage from the old self to the new creation.

We need only look around us with faith to see this mystery unfolding in the lives of others. It is like seeing the world with a new set of eyes. We are no longer watching suffering in its futility or pain without meaning. We are witnesses of the resurrection as it emerges in the lives of searching people:

- a young mother who gives selflessly to her children during sleepless nights and long days.

- an old man who is dying of cancer and knows that he will not see his family again.

- a lonely widow who cannot forget the companionship of her husband and has found no way to fill the darkness of her life.

In each of these lives there is a set of outer circumstances that can be recorded and put on file. But these external facts do not reveal the real truth about their lives. The search for God and the search for meaning goes on quietly within them. It is an inward quest that will lead them to despair or to hope. It can be an empty groping without meaning or direction, or it can be a journey toward life, signed with the Spirit and sealed with hope. It can be a night flight toward oblivion or a participation in the paschal mystery of the Lord.

We participate in the paschal journey of Christ each time we commit ourselves to faithful self-giving. We share in his journey each time we acknowledge our need for hope at a moment of helplessness. We make the mystery of salvation present in our lives each time our hunger for God is too immense for our hearts. We encounter the risen Lord in the epiphanies and breakthroughs, the tears and laughter of our daily search.

We share the way of Christ when we experience ourselves as challenged beyond our capacity or stretched beyond our strength. We walk in the new exodus when we break out of the fears that immobilize us or reaffirm the covenant of honesty in the silence of our hearts. The pasch of the Lord is traced in our flesh each time we choose to hope, each time we choose to walk an extra mile, each time we drink the cup of suffering, each time we share our pain or our joy.

Following the Lord toward Life

To grow, a lobster must shed its old shell numerous times. Each shedding renders the creature totally defenseless until the new shell forms.

Human beings do not live under water or have a protective shell comparable to that of the lobster, but we do know the pain, the fear, and the risk of continual growth. In his letters Paul often speaks of this struggle toward growth in his own life. He knew well what it meant to lose all his defenses and to find himself suddenly helpless in the ruins of his life. He also knew what it meant to be raised up by God in order to begin a new life.

"I am far from being perfect," he writes to the Phillipians, "I have not yet won. But I am still running, trying to capture the prize for which Christ Jesus captured me. I can assure you, my brothers and sisters, I am far from thinking that I have already won. All I can say is that I forget the past and strain ahead for what is still to come. I am racing for the finish, for the prize to which God calls us upwards to receive in Christ Jesus" (Phillipians 3:10-15).

Forgetting the past in order to "strain ahead" toward the future is never easy. It involves risk and resurrection, death and rebirth. The past can trap us in a quagmire of guilt or failure. It can hold us prisoner in a world of nostalgia and lost dreams. It can lull us into mediocrity.

Christianity lives on a promise. It offers us the faithful vision of Jesus who did not cling to security, but emptied himself to become a servant. In the letting go, there was risk. In the rising, there was promise. In his straining toward the future, Jesus has become the *prodromos*—the forerunner who has gone before us into fulfillment(cf He 6:20). He has finished the course. He has won the race. He has become perfect.

Few of us fully understand the immediate call to growth in our lives. We flail about in our sleep. We cling to yesterday. We are not sure of the road. We are far from being perfect. We have not yet won.

But we are still running.

CHAPTER TWO

Running Away

"But Jonah decided to run away from Yahweh, and to go to Tarshish."

—Jonah 1:2

IT was still dark when the clock radio clicked on. At first the melody of the music was lost in the oblivion of sleep. Then, somewhere in my subconscious, there was a clash of realities. On a stopwatch it would have been only a few seconds, but in the suspended time of semi-sleep I passed through several levels of confusion on my way toward consciousness.

What is that sound? What is this place? Where am I? Then, recognition: It is morning. I am in my room. It's time to get up. Followed by denial: It's too early. I need more sleep. Push the snooze alarm. Roll over and go back to sleep.

I opened my eyes to confirm what my instinct had been telling me. Through the window I saw a dark sky and the bare outline of trees. It was raining. Yes, it was morning. The grey light and the slow drizzle made the bed a refuge of warmth and security.

In a flash the day's agenda swept through my mind—the unfinished business, the appointments, the needs, the demands, the promise, and the pain. For a few moments I weighed the alternatives and pulled the blankets tightly around me. Then I sat upright on the edge of the bed. Partly out of instinct, partly out of free decision, I stood up, stretched, and began to move toward another day.

Waking Up To Life

The ordinary carries mystery like the soil bears a seed—quietly and with the commonness of a grey dawn. There is an invitation to faith even in a clock radio's morning music. Each morning we grope our way toward consciousness. Each day we are stunned by the light. We hesitate at the edge of our bed, caught for a moment in that most basic of choices—to rise to life or to turn back toward sleep.

Waking up is a metaphor for life. It is a model for the life-time process of growing in faith. The rhythm of sleeping and waking is a daily reminder of the paschal mystery which unfolds through the ebb and flow of our seasons.

Initially the call of God is indistinct and confused. It is a vague awareness beneath the surface of our lives. In the gradual growth toward maturity the call becomes clearer and more insistent. Like the dawn of a new day, the summons of faith is both threatening and inviting, demanding and consoling. The final response is in our hands. We must decide whether or not we will follow the call

toward transformation or turn aside and dwell in darkness. When we turn toward the light we are choosing the path that Jesus walked before us.

Holiness is a process of becoming whole through the power of his Spirit. The journey toward wholeness is long and arduous and we do not always choose the way that leads toward life. We do not always recognize those things that would be "for our peace" (Lk 19:42).

Metanoia or Paranoia?

"Be converted and believe in the good news!" With this proclamation Jesus began his public ministry. His message was clear: This is the turning point of history. The kingdom of God is among you. Wake up! Change your way of viewing life and your way of living it.

This is not the kind of message that can be easily ignored. It is like the insistent sound of an alarm clock in the morning. We must either open ourselves to the gospel and be transformed by its power, or we must choose to flee from its demands.

The biblical word for turning toward the good news is *metanoia*—conversion. Metanoia literally means a change of mind, but it implies far more than a rational process of changing our mental attitude. Metanoia describes a radical transformation of our inner self. In the experience of conversion we break through to a new self-understanding. We discover that the relationship between God and ourselves is no longer able to be contained in rules and external ritual. It becomes a covenant written in the "fleshy tablets of the heart" (Jr 31:33) and inscribed in the depth of our being.

Moral theologians sometimes speak of conversion as "a joyful change of heart." In the final choice to turn toward God there may well be a surge of joy, but initially metanoia is often a threatening experience. The call to conversion is threatening because it demands that we let go of our desire to control life on our terms. It implies that we are willing to move out of our self-centered world to follow Christ in his passage through death to new life. It requires that we abandon the false self and embrace the authentic self created in God's image. It means that we are willing to walk away from illusion toward the consuming truth of the gospel.

Before we can embrace the gospel as good news it is often necessary to experience it as bad news. At the turning points of our lives the implications of faith race through our minds like the agenda for a busy day. We hesitate for a while at the edge of life.

We are faced with the ancient ambiguity—to rise to new life or to lapse back into sleep. In our fear we often choose to run away rather than to respond, to hide rather than to step forward.

The opposite of conversion is aversion. The other side of metanoia is *paranoia*. Paranoia is usually understood in psychological terms. It is characterized by fear, suspicion and flight from reality. Paranoia usually results in elaborate illusions and self-deception.

In the biblical context paranoia implies more than an emotional or mental imbalance. It refers to an attitude of being, a stance of the heart. Spiritual paranoia is the flight from God and from one's true self. It is the attempt to escape from responsibility. It is the tendency to avoid the cost of discipleship and to seek out an escape route from the demands of Christianity. Paranoia of the spirit is characterized by an attempt to deny the reality of the gospel or to distort it in such a way that we rationalize our behavior and choose our own way.

Christians are not exempt from this human struggle. If anything, they find the stakes of life raised even higher. Christians are people who struggle to turn their fears into love, their flight into the free response of faith. They walk the narrow ridge between responsibility and selling out, between hope and despair, fidelity and betrayal. They live in the tension between metanoia and paranoia.

Running Away: The Sign of Jonah

After Thomas Merton had been at the Trappist monastery of Gethsemani for ten years he published his journal under the title, *The Sign of Jonah.* The book is a series of reflections on his search for God in solitude and prayer.

But why the title? What did Merton's conversion to Catholicism and his first years as a monk have to do with the figure of Jonah?

Tradition sees Jonah as the symbol of rebirth and transformation. In the history of religious art Jonah is pictured as a forerunner of Christ's resurrection. This is the context in which Jesus himself spoke of the Old Testament prophet. When the Pharisees demanded a sign to justify his claims, Jesus responded with these words: "It is an evil and unfaithful generation that asks for a sign! The only sign it will be given is the sign of the prophet Jonah. For as Jonah was in the belly of the sea-monster for three days and three nights, so will the Son of man be in the heart of the earth for three days and three nights" (Mt 12:39–40).

What is the sign of Jonah? It is the proclamation that through God's power life overcomes death. The human heart can be transformed. Rebirth is possible. Merton understood his conversion to Catholicism and his decision to enter the Trappist community as a personal experience of the sign of Jonah. To the amazement of his friends and associates Merton's life had been transformed by the call of God. His vision had been expanded beyond his imagining.

Merton reflects on this transformation in these words: "The sign Jesus promised to the generation that did not understand him was the 'sign of Jonah the prophet'—that is, the sign of his own resurrection. The life of every monk, of every priest, of every Christian is signed with the sign of Jonah, because we all live by the power of Christ's resurrection."

Just as Jesus was a source of bewilderment for

the Pharisees, so the experience of personal renewal in a Christian's life is often a sign of contradiction to non-believers. Merton saw his monastic
vocation as a share in this sign of transformation.

But there is another way to understand the sign
of Jonah. It is true that Jonah became a symbol of
rebirth and a sign of conversion. But this was not
always the case. In the beginning Jonah was a re-
luctant prophet. He resisted God's call to take the
message of salvation to a foreign nation. When
God summoned him to set out for Nineveh, he
refused to go. Instead he boarded a ship going in
the opposite direction toward Tarshish.

The sign of Jonah, therefore, is a symbol of resistance as much as it is a sign of rebirth. It
speaks of paranoia as well as metanoia. It is a sign
of the struggle against the implications of God's
call in our lives.

Thomas Merton experienced this same tension
of faith. He recognized that the ambiguity of his
life continued after his conversion and his solemn
commitment to religious life. "Before becoming a
priest," Merton observes, "I had made a great
fuss about solitude and had been rather a nuisance to my superiors and directors in my aspirations for a solitary life. Now, after my ordination,
I discovered that the essence of a solitary vocation is that it is a vocation to fear, to helplessness,
to isolation in the invisible God."

Conversion does not take away our inward
struggle with fear. Faith does not dispel all doubt.
The sign of Jonah is a sign of contradiction for

ourselves as well as for those around us. In the wake of rebirth we are still faced with the temptation to flee from God.

In the Belly Of a Paradox

The impact of Merton's writings lies at least partially in his honesty and forthrightness. His life grew more deeply toward God because he accepted the shadow as well as the light of his inner self. He reminds us that the process of personal purification is long and painful. In the prologue of his journal, Merton makes this statement: "Like the prophet Jonah, whom God ordered to go to Nineveh, I found myself with an almost uncontrollable desire to go in the opposite direction. God pointed one way and all my 'ideals' pointed in the other. . . . Like Jonah himself I find myself traveling toward my destiny in the belly of a paradox."

In the paschal mystery the sign of Jonah was transformed into the sign of Jesus. The brokenness was healed, the flight reversed. Jesus did not turn and run. He did not resist the Father's call or reject the road that led to Jerusalem.

Neither did he remove the ambiguity of our lives. Jesus conquered death but he did not save us from dying. Jesus broke the bonds of darkness but he did not rescue us from fear. He did not dispel the paradox of being human. Our pilgrimage toward life is patterned after the Lord's dying and rising. Suffering is part of the cost of discipleship. Each day we must pick up the cross of our blindness and brokenness and carry it forward. Like Merton, we find ourselves traveling toward our destiny in the belly of a paradox.

How can we move toward deeper conversion? What are the fears that control our lives? What are the patterns of paranoia in us? How are we running from God and from life?

Adam and Eve: Flight from Responsibility

Theologians have traditionally interpreted the first sin as one of rebellion. The serpent promised Adam and Eve that they would "become like gods." This appears to be an obvious appeal to pride, an invitation to become something more than human.

But the Genesis account suggests another way of looking at sin. This perspective is based on the consequences which flow from the choices which our first parents made rather than the apparent attitudes with which they carried them out. From this point of view sin is primarily an abdication of responsibility. Before Eve rebels against God by eating from the tree, she has already abandoned her position of human leadership by giving the serpent control over her decisions. The flight from responsibility is even clearer in the response which Adam and Eve make to their decision. First, they hide from each other and from God. Later, when Yahweh confronts them, they blame the serpent.

Mental anguish, social pressures, childhood trauma, emotional illness, boredom—all of these are contemporary versions of the ancient tendency to blame something or someone outside ourselves. "The devil made me do it"—it was Adam and Eve's excuse, and it is often ours today. Harvey Cox contends that "man's most debilitating proclivity is not his pride. It is not his attempt to be more than man. Rather it is his sloth, his unwillingness to be everything man was intended to be."

Perhaps our sin is not so much our desire to be like gods, as it is our refusal to become fully human. The Genesis story explores the tendency to "leave it to the snake." It describes our unwillingness to be responsible for creation and for ourselves. In our refusal to accept this responsibility we are rejecting the dignity to which we have been called. We are choosing to be subservient to forces outside ourselves.

The Jewish people observed the passover meal as a banquet of freedom. They celebrated God's call to leave behind the idols and the bricks of Pharaoh. The passover is a reminder that at one, decisive moment in their lives they were more willing to become wayfarers in the desert than slaves in Egypt.

Jesus understood his life as the new passover. He measured his life in the light of freedom. "The Father loves me," he told his disciples, "because I lay down my life in order to take it up again. No one takes it from me. I lay it down of my own free will, and as it is in my power to lay it down, so it is in my power to take it up again" (Jn 10:17-18).

The flight from accountability is a paranoid response to life. It is the decision to withdraw from the cost of discipleship and the burden of the cross. It is the refusal to follow the Lord in his paschal mystery.

Cain: Flight from the Center

> *Things fall apart; the center cannot hold;*
> *Mere anarchy is loosed upon the world.*

These lines from Yeats' poem, "The Second Coming," give us a brief, but striking description of human life alienated from its source. When we abdicate our responsibility to God and to our world the stability of our lives is lost. Relationships fall apart. The center cannot hold.

The Genesis story pictures Eden as the center of the earth. This is intended to be a spiritual image rather than a geographical description. Adam and Eve stand at the center of creation. They find their roots and the source of their meaning in God. When the pair reject Yahweh as the center of their lives, the result, in Yeats' words, is "anarchy loosed upon the world."

When the Genesis account is read in its entirety it provides a sweeping panorama of the consequences of sin and human irresponsibility. In Cain the broken center erupts in jealousy, violence, and finally murder. Like Adam and Eve, Cain refuses to be responsible. " 'Where is your brother,' Yahweh asked Cain. 'I do not know,' he replied. 'Am I my brother's keeper?' " (Gn 4:9).

In the experience of Cain the broken center of creation is further fragmented. Adam and Eve hid from God. Cain goes beyond hiding. He flees across the face of the earth, burdened with guilt and marked with the sign of fear. In Cain, humanity becomes "a fugitive and a wanderer over the earth" (Gn 4:14). Original sin is another way of saying that we are born into a world that has lost its center. Like Cain we find ourselves living "east of Eden."

Jesus is our way back to the center. His dying and rising turn our wandering into a journey toward life, our paranoia into metanoia. To be a disciple of the Lord is to discover that the slaves have been set free and the fugitives have become pilgrims of the Spirit.

The Prodigal Son: Flight from Community

Jesus' stories of compassion and mercy usually take the form of a search for that which is lost or a journey in search of life. Thus in Luke's gospel we have the parables of the lost sheep, the lost drachma, and the prodigal son (cf. Lk 15).

The story of the prodigal is, in some ways, a summary of the brokenness of the human condition. There is something essentially attractive about the younger son. He is adventurous and willing to take risks. In contrast to his older brother, the younger son is restless and searching for a new experience of life. He is by instinct a seeker rather than a settler.

In reality, however, his journey is less a searching than it is a flight—a running away from reality and human relationships. His story recapitulates the other biblical stories of flight. The prodigal is Adam and Eve hiding from God. He is Cain the fugitive. He is Jonah on the run. On the surface he is taking his inheritance to go in search of life. In reality he is leaving his roots, abandoning his center, to seek life on his own terms. He is searching for a world of self-centered experience, a kingdom of things and passing relationships which he mistakenly believes will fulfill him.

The figure of the prodigal son can be seen today in the emerging cult of personality and individualism. If the sixties were characterized by the commune and the quest for togetherness, the seventies and eighties may well be remembered as the decades of individualism.

The cult of individualism is present wherever there is the flight from authentic relationships. It is found wherever people demand happiness on their own terms. Most often the result is an encounter with futility. When we trade convenience for commitment we find ourselves in the lonely world of the prodigal. Individualism is a subtle form of paranoia. Under the guise of seeking, it is in reality a flight from community and from God.

A Bundle of Contradictions

Few people in the history of Christianity have experienced as dramatic a conversion as Saul of Tarsus. In the Acts of the Apostles there are no less than three separate accounts of Paul's encounter with the risen Lord. This gives us some indication of the importance which Paul and the early church attached to this event. Obviously the conversion experience was a definitive turning point in Paul's life.

But it would be a mistake to isolate this breakthrough from the rest of his spiritual journey. The transformation of Saul the pharisee into Paul the apostle did not happen overnight. Like every other Christian, Paul faced the mystery of his personal darkness and the contradictions of his daily life.

In his letter to the Christians at Rome, Paul acknowledges that the challenge to live the Christian life is far from easy. He speaks of his continual spiritual struggle with the same honesty with which he described his earlier conversion:

I don't understand what I do. It's not what I really want that I do, but what I hate—that's what I do. . . . I'm finding out that goodness doesn't stay long in my natural self, because I have strength enough to want to do good but not enough to actually do it. (Rm 7:15, 18).

We tend to identify the success or failure of our lives with the major choices and turning points in our spiritual journey. The decisions regarding a career, a place to live, and our life-time relationships loom large on the horizon. We spend time in prayer weighing the alternatives, testing our resolve, and stretching our vision. Usually there are unanswered questions and areas of doubt. But at a certain point we know that we must choose. In the face of ambiguity and darkness we act. We walk a new road. We claim a new responsibility.

The search to find a direction in life is not always fought on such an epic scale. More often it is lived out in the daily tension of accepting our brokenness or of being faithful to our work and our relationships. Routine is another word for the testing ground of our lives. Like Paul, we discover that the major decisions must be enfleshed in the daily struggle between courage and cowardice.

In her diary Anne Frank speaks of this ambiguity with sensitivity and insight. "They haven't given me the name 'little bundle of contradictions' for nothing," she writes. "I have, as it were, a dual personality . . . the first is . . . all the unpleasant qualities for which I'm renowned. The second nobody knows about, that is my secret. . . you must realize that no one knows Anne's better side and that's why most people find me so insufferable. . . . I keep trying to find a way of becoming what I would so like to be, and what I could be, if . . . there weren't any other people in the world."

Anne Frank's reflections echo the words and the experience of Paul. She is describing the tension between metanoia and paranoia in the setting of everyday emotions and the search for self-identity. The awareness that we are "a bundle of contradictions" is a common experience for all of us. It is in facing this truth that self-knowledge begins. When we confront our contradictions we recognize that we are not yet whole. We acknowledge our divided hearts. We know that we are pilgrims.

But the road we walk is destined for glory. When we accept our ambiguity we also celebrate that the Spirit is at work in us—leading us through our contradictions toward eternal life.

CHAPTER THREE

Wandering

"They shall wander from sea to sea,
   and from north to east;
They shall run to and fro, to seek the
   Word of the Lord,
   but they shall not find it."
                    —Amos 8:2 (RSV)

"MAY I have your attention please! Because of fog and poor visibility all flights have been temporarily canceled. Stand by for further information. I repeat, all flights have been canceled."

I was standing in line to have my bags checked when the announcement came. An audible groan went through the crowded terminal. It was followed by a flurry of questions and a general state of confusion. The airport was teeming with holiday travelers. Some of them scrambled to find a telephone. Others jostled their way toward the ticket counters to arrange for new flight connections. Some went in search of empty seats or to find something to read. Others stayed in line with the hope that the delay would be brief. After a half-hour, however, it became clear that "temporarily" might mean several hours.

The airport settled into a psychic holding pattern. The cocktail bars and the coffee shops were filled to capacity. The newsstands and the gift shops were doing a brisk business. I threaded my way through the crowd in search of a place to wait. By now all the available seats had been taken. I finally found a space near the windows next to a middle-aged man in a business suit. I converted my suitcase into a make-shift chair and sat down to watch the crowds.

"Where are you headed?" the man asked, attempting to initiate a conversation.

"Minneapolis," I responded, "I'm on my way back from a meeting."

"The fog is really thick," he mused. "We could be in for a long wait."

We exchanged a few more sentences and then lapsed into silence. As I watched the faces of those who were passing by, the man's question became a collective one. Where are they headed? Where are all these people going? Back from a business trip? Away on a vacation? Home for the holidays? On the first leg of a journey to Europe?

I realized that I was viewing only a small part of the people who were affected by the adverse weather. In my mind's eye I pictured the others whom I could not see: the air traffic controllers studying their radar screens or taking a coffee break; the ground crews standing by with baggage and fuel; the pilots and airline personnel in their lounges. Wherever we were going we shared one thing in common: we were waiting—waiting

to take off, waiting to land, waiting to say good-bye, waiting to say hello.

Slowly, in the fog-shrouded terminal, surrounded by strangers, something came clear to me. There is some reason for this delay. In the world of faith there are no pure accidents. Waiting is more than a circumstance; it is an invitation to explore the truth.

A Different Kind of Destination

Where are you headed? The businessman's question moved me toward a deeper level of reflection. I wondered how many other people in the terminal had been asked that same question. Like me they probably answered by sharing the obvious information. The computer had printed a set of data on their tickets—electronic abbreviations for places and people: New Orleans, San Francisco, New York, Tampa, St. Louis.

For a few hours, however, we were not going to any of the destinations listed. The weather had changed the timetable of our lives. Suddenly we were face to face with each other and with ourselves. In the attempt to pass time or distract ourselves we might miss the invitation of this moment.

Where are you headed? For now the question was not related to our tickets or to our baggage claim checks. It had nothing to do with the place of departure or the port of arrival. It was a question directed toward the inward direction of our lives. Where are we going as people and pilgrims?

What is the shape of our destiny, the pattern of our search? Where is home?

I looked at the faces of those who walked past with renewed interest and compassion. There was a young coed dressed in the latest fashion; a bearded man in a cashmere coat; a young couple walking hand in hand; a middle-aged mother clutching the hands of her children; an older woman with sad eyes. Where were they going with their lives? What was the shape of their dreams? What kind of choices were they making for their lives?

Some of those in the terminal had left home to begin a new life. Others were going back to their roots with the realization that they had no home—only shattered dreams and broken relationships. Some were in emotional and spiritual holding patterns—enmeshed in their work, lost in the pursuit of a career, flailing at the future in search of fulfillment.

Perhaps there were some in the terminal who had experienced a turning point in their lives. They waited now to respond to the call and to walk forward with courage. Some, I knew, were simply circling in a fog, neither running away nor coming home. They were like the incoming aircraft, operating on instruments, without feeling and without seeing a direction.

Where Are You Headed?

I turned toward the window and stared again at the fog that enveloped the airport. The outer weather was no clearer than the inner. I was aware that I had been lost in thought for some time. All the while I had been wondering about *their* direction and *their* meaning. What about my own? Where was I going? What is the pattern of my pilgrimage? What choices were shaping the destiny of my life?

For a moment the external circumstances did not matter. The ticket which I carried in my coat pocket was of no help. The real destination of my life was inside me, waiting to be shaped by freedom and enfleshed by commitment.

Two hours later I walked onto the airplane. The fog was beginning to lift. The instruments of technology declared that the weather was clear enough for flying. We took off into what remained of the fog and then flew above the clouds into clear sky. As the plane banked toward the west I could see the sun sinking toward the horizon. For now at least I could say that I was going home.

For a few hours I had shared a moment of awareness with strangers. I could not remember their faces now. I would not recognize them if they passed me in a new place. All the same, we had shared something significant. We had experienced the passage of time and the awareness of inner space. As the plane flew toward the night I was aware that every experience carves out a mystery which cannot be contained by circumstances. Every encounter is part of a greater mystery. Every moment is rooted in a deeper journey—the passage of the Lord through our lives.

Wandering

The long afternoon which I spent waiting in an airport has remained with me as more than a memory. It has become a symbol of the psychic and spiritual holding patterns we sometimes choose for our lives.

There are seasons in our lives when there is a clear sense of direction. We look at the future with clarity and move toward it with confidence. But there are also darker seasons. There are times when our fears cloud the horizon and we lose our way. Instead of moving toward life, we begin to run away from life. Sometimes our flight takes us into the wasteland of personal isolation. At other times we seek shelter in the amnesia of work, job performance, or routine. Sometimes we simply choose to stop feeling altogether and allow a sense of oblivion to pervade our lives.

After awhile this tendency toward withdrawal can become a way of life. We begin to live each day as though there were no purpose in life other than avoiding anybody or any event which would invite us into deeper dialogue. We would rather face the void than risk the pain of growth. We would rather submit to boredom than face the demands of change. We would rather be controlled by our circumstances than set out toward a new land.

Scripture gives this aimless pattern of the heart a name. It calls it "wandering." This term describes the futile pathway of those who find it too difficult to trust God or life. Wandering is what Adam and Eve did after their flight from God. It is the way Cain lived out his life in the land of Nod. It is the feeling of futility which Qoheleth describes in his lament about human life. Wandering is what we experience whenever we choose to live in the bleak world that lies "east of Eden."

Nowhere is the theme of wandering more graphically portrayed than in the story of the Israelites' journey toward the promised land. In its initial stages the Hebrews experienced the exodus as a dramatic liberation from slavery and a promise of a land to call their own. Their throats were filled with battle cries and the songs of victory. But the spirit of elation was short-lived. With Egypt and the Sea of Reeds behind them, the Israelites now turned their faces toward the desert. They were confronted with a howling wasteland where there was no food or water, no landmarks and, to all appearances, no future.

Their first reaction was to complain bitterly to Moses and Aaron: "Why did we not die at Yahweh's hand in the land of Egypt, when we were able to sit down to pans of meat and could eat bread to our heart's content? As it is, you have brought us to this wilderness to starve this whole company to death!" (Ex 16:3).

"Grumbling" is the threshold to wandering. The murmuring of the people is the first step toward years of aimlessness in the wilderness. There is a strange irony in all of this. Even though the Lord fed the Israelites with manna and quail and gave them living water from the desert rocks,

they still continued to complain against him.
Even though he went before them with a pillar of
cloud by day and a pillar of fire by night, they
kept on murmuring.

This inward attitude of mistrust had outward
consequences. As the hearts of the people became
more hardened and stubborn, their journey became more aimless. For forty years they wan-
dered through the desert in search of the land
which Yahweh had promised them.

The desert journey is a symbol of our own
search for life. It is a striking profile of our own
spiritual and emotional holding patterns. What
begins as a journey toward life can easily become
a trek toward oblivion. That which we initially
hear as a call to freedom can, through our fear and
mistrust, become a self-imposed experience of
slavery. Wandering is another word for refusing
to grow. It is a different way of describing the tendency to give up on life and to settle for a slow
death. Whenever we choose the pathway of withdrawal, we trade adventure for false security. We
may well find ourselves circling in a wilderness
that is void of life, a desert marked only with our
own desperate footprints.

Wanderers are pilgrims who have sold out; they
are poets who have stopped singing; seers without a vision.

Adam, Where Are You?

We may withdraw from God, but he will not
abandon us. That is the promise which God
makes to his people—a promise which we see ful-

filled in the person of Jesus. We may choose a pattern of wandering, but God continues to prod us toward life. He continues to seek us out with compassion. He pursues us with his love.

We are accustomed to think of human beings as the restless seekers of creation. We acknowledge that it is human to ask questions and to search for meaning. We are familiar, for instance, with the figure of Job questioning God about the mystery of suffering and the issue of justice. We recognize the plaintive questions of the psalms and their pleas for God's intervention.

In light of this, it may surprise us to learn that the first question in the bible is posed not by human beings but by God: "Adam, where are you?"(cf Gn 3:9). The creator comes in search of his creature. The divine potter seeks out the clay vessel which he shaped from the earth and into which he breathed his spirit.

Adam, where are you? In posing this question it is clear that Yahweh is not looking for a report on Adam's physical whereabouts. God is not particularly interested in what tree or rock Adam and Eve are using for a hiding place. He *is* interested, however, in the fact that they are hiding; that they have withdrawn from the source of life into a state of alienation. We might rephrase God's question to read: "Adam, what's going on in your life? Where are you in your journey?"

The sacred writer's insight into human nature is revealed in a striking way in this passage. He indicates that before God went for his customary walk in the twilight; before he asked about

Adam's whereabouts, the man and the woman were already aware that something was wrong. "The eyes of both of them were opened and they realized that they were naked. So they sewed fig leaves together to make themselves loin-cloths. The man and his wife heard the sound of Yahweh God walking in the garden in the cool of the day, and they hid from Yahweh God among the trees of the garden"(Gn 3:7-8).

In its healthiest form, guilt is like an early-warning device which tells us that all is not well. It is an instinctive signal telling us that we have lost touch with life; that we have fragmented the primordial harmony established by God. In Gabriel Marcel's words, guilt is a "dis-ease"—a sense of being alienated from the truth and from ourselves.

Adam, where are you? God's question merely reflects the obvious uneasiness which is already present in his creatures. It is not intended to be an accusation. It is a question of concern rather than condemnation. God's light illumines our lives in order that we might find our way back to peace. The chaotic world which we create by our attempt to grasp at knowledge is healed by divine love. Human brokenness is answered by divine compassion. Into our holding patterns and our hiding places God comes in search of us. We may not experience his nearness in any dramatic way. We may hear no sound except our own voice and the voices of people around us. We may see nothing that we have not seen before. But the Lord is near to us all the same. We recognize his call in the undying hunger of our hearts for meaning. We sense his persistent love in our restlessness—the uneasiness which tells us that we have traded the journey for an aimless wandering.

Adam, where are you? We might not want to hear that question. We may even try to block it out by increasing the level of activity or by seeking to immerse ourselves in other distractions. But the question will not go away. It will emerge from the emptiness of our hearts. It will arise out of the deep recesses of our lives. Just as it arose, long ago, in the life of a crippled man, who waited at the pool of Bethsaida.

Do You Want To Get Well?

For years the crippled man had been lost in the crowd. In a courtyard filled with the disabled and the forgotten, he was just another face in the crowd. It had been a long time since anyone had even noticed him. The days came and went with the same emptiness and waiting. The months and the years unfolded in an unchanging pattern. He had watched many people come to the pool, be healed in its waters, and then leave. But he was still here. His life appeared to be a gesture of futility, a watch without dawn, a waiting without hope.

But today the Rabbi was looking at him. There was compassion in his eyes and gentleness in his hands. Jesus gazed at him steadily and asked: "Do you want to be healed?"

At first the crippled man was stunned by this

question. After all the years of waiting one would think that the answer to this question was obvious. Why did Jesus ask it? Was there any doubt? Is it possible that someone would not want to be healed?

The answer is yes. There are some people who give up on themselves and on life. There are some who do not want to get well, who choose not to be healed. Healing is God's work, but it cannot take place without the desire and decision of the sick person. Holiness is the Father's gift, but it can only be received into hearts that are hungry for love.

Do you want to be healed? It is a question that endures long after its original response. It is a question that is addressed to us at the turning points of our lives. Do you want to begin again? Are you willing to risk growth and change?

Like the crippled man we wait for the waters of life to move. We watch for an invitation to wholeness. And usually there are dimensions of ourselves that resist change. At times we cling to brokenness because it is safer. We are afraid of the risk and the insecurity of radical change. We would rather limp in a familiar world than leap in the darkness. We are willing to risk some dimensions of our lives, but we find it painfully difficult to let go and trust God.

Do you want to get well? Those who have experienced chemical dependency know that they must confront this question before anything else can happen. Those who are paralyzed by emotional fears know that they too must face it. In one way or another we must all answer this question. Even if we recognize our need for healing, we cannot begin to change until we choose to get help.

The crippled man needed help to get into the pool and it was there in the person of Jesus. But there is something powerful in this man that transcends his physical helplessness. It is his undying hope. For thirty-eight years he had clung to life like a flame in darkness. He never lost his desire to be healed. He never lost his will to live. When Jesus came to him, he was still watching in hope. He still wanted to be made whole.

This time it was different. When the waters moved, he was in them. He walked away from the courtyard and the temple. He walked through the city streets and into the countryside. Somewhere along the road he praised God by leaping in the sunlight.

CHAPTER FOUR

Turning Around

"When he came to himself he said 'How many of my father's hired servants have bread enough and to spare, but I perish here with hunger! I will arise and go to my father . . .'"

—Luke 15:17-18(RSV)

LONG ago, in a far away country, the citizens discovered a small amount of a very precious metal. The news spread rapidly throughout the land. There was excitement everywhere. The king called a meeting of his counselors to decide what should be done with the precious substance. Would they use the metal to mint new coins? Would they convert it into jewelry for the royal family? Or would they use it to make swords and weapons for war?

After the discussion had gone on for several hours the king interrupted and said: "This metal is too precious and too beautiful to be used for any personal or competitive purpose. It should be shared with all the people of the kingdom. We shall commission the leading artist in our country to create a sculpture out of the precious metal.

The work of art will be placed in the city square as a symbol of our nation's vision."

And so it happened. The king summoned the most renowned sculptor in the land and told him about the plans. The artist agreed to take on the project. He took the precious metal with him and immediately set to work. For three years he labored in his studio with little sleep or food. He worked long into the night creating the design and casting the mold.

After the artist had finished his work the king called for a great festival to unveil the statue. The crowds gathered. The bands played. There were parades and speeches. Finally the solemn moment arrived. Before a vast crowd of people the king himself unveiled the work of art. There was a moment of awe-filled silence and then thunderous applause. The crowds were thrilled with the beauty and grace of the statue. The counselors nodded their approval. The king beamed with pride. Everyone was happy.

Everyone, that is, except the artist. He stood at the edge of the crowd with tears in his eyes. "Why are you sad?" the king asked him. "The statue is beautiful beyond words. Clearly you see that the people are proud and pleased. Why are you weeping?"

"I am sad because there is no more of the precious metal," the artist replied. "I have never worked with such beautiful material. Inside of me there is an energy and a vision that still waits to be born, a fire that needs to be expressed. I weep because I know that I will never be satisfied un-

less I melt this statue down and start over again."

"But you have already created a masterpiece," the king insisted, "why to you want to destroy it?"

The artist paused for a moment. He looked at the statue and then at the king. When he spoke his voice was quiet and edged with intensity: "I must melt it down because the act of creating is more important to me than the finished work of art. I must express my vision or I will die."

Conversion: On Being Melted Down

In some mysterious way we all resemble the artist in this story. God gives us a precious amount of life—our share in the journey of existence. He invites us to create our vision and our destiny. Since each of us is unique and irreplaceable, we cannot live someone else's life or ask them to live ours. The limits of our historical circumstances and the constant flow of time tell us that there is only a small amount of experience that we can call our own. That is the precious metal of our life. Through it we must try to express our vision.

Like the artist we realize that the creative response is more important than any stage of growth that we might attain. We are never finished with the task of shaping our freedom and future. "I live on Earth at present," writes Buckminister Fuller, "and I don't know what I am. I know that I am not a category. I am not a thing—a noun. I seem to be a verb, an evolutionary process." We are not still-life pictures, but life-in-process. We are sculptors, not statues.

Nevertheless, there are times when we are tempted to stand back from our lives and refuse to create. There are at least two moments when we would rather turn our back on life and become part of the crowd. One is the moment of failure. The other is the moment of success. In the first there is a temptation toward despair. In the second there is a tendency toward self-complacence. Although we may not realize it, the moments of brokenness and the times of breakthrough both carry a challenge to let go and to begin anew. They are invitations to trust the flow of our lives and to touch new sources of creativity within us.

Conversion is another word for our willingness to turn toward new life. It is that moment when we are willing to be "melted down" in order to begin anew. Conversion takes place in many different ways and circumstances. It might express itself in our willingness to turn away from a broken life and to turn toward the gospel. It might be realized in our commitment to grow more deeply in the divine life that is already within us. Conversion is not only for sinners. It is for saints. It is the recurring call to let go of the past and to move toward the future.

Are We the Sculptors of Our Lives?

On the surface it appears that the responsibility for conversion is in our hands. Human experience seems to indicate that life is simply the outcome of our choices—or lack of them. God has given us the precious metal of life. "Trade till I come (Lk 19:13)," he tells us. Create until I return. Shape yourselves and your future.

Or Is God?

The notion that the self is the sculptor of freedom is rooted in our everyday experience of responsibility. But this is a limited perspective. With the eyes of faith we move toward a more encompassing view of human life. In the biblical framework our creativity is rooted in God. He is the divine artist and we are simply sharers in his creative act. We are clay before we are potters. We are shaped before we are able to shape our world. We are created before we become creative.

Genesis pictures God as the primordial artist who forms human beings out of the clay of the earth. He breathes into the clay and it becomes a living being—an icon of its maker. We carry within us the breath of Yahweh, the spark of the divine, the power to know, to choose, and to shape our lives and our world.

God is not a distant Lord who creates us and then retreats into the far reaches of the universe. He is nearer to us than our breath, more intimate than our hearts. His creative presence continues to shape, to heal, to restore, and to sanctify our lives. "House of Israel," Yahweh asks his people, "can I not do to you what the potter does? Yes, as the clay is in the potter's hands, so you are in mine" (Jr 18:6).

Redemption in Christ is literally a reshaping of

our broken lives. It is a re—creation, a rebirth to new life. The breath of God which we share is the Holy Spirit given to us by the risen Lord. "For anyone who is in Christ," writes St. Paul, "there is a new creation" (II Cor 5:17). Even though we carry the divine life in "earthenware jars" we are, by our calling, capable of radical transformation. In the mystery of salvation God continues to shape our lives in love. The human journey is a creative tension between God's call and our response, between God's providence and our freedom.

The Pattern of Conversion

Conversion is the biblical way of describing the ever-deepening process of turning toward God. It is *metanoia* (the decision to turn toward life) rather than *paranoia* (the choice to run from life). Conversion is not something that we can accomplish on our own. Without the initiative of the Holy Spirit within us we would not have the courage or the strength to leave behind our failures or to "melt down" our successes and turn more deeply toward God.

The biblical meaning of conversion implies personal transformation. In the current of daily living there is a subtle tendency to conform ourselves to the patterns of culture. The pressures of advertising and the media invite us to invest in a consumerist view of life and to sell out on the Christian vision. In this sense, conversion is a creative act of defiance. It is our refusal, in Kierkegaard's words, to become part of "the crowd." "Do not conform yourself to this age," writes St. Paul, "but be transformed by the renewal of your mind" (Rm 12:2).

Bernard Lonergan points out that this inner transformation of life can take three forms: (1) a radical change of heart (religious conversion); (2) a new way of looking at ourselves and our world (intellectual conversion); (3) a major shift in our personal values (moral conversion).

Do these various forms of conversion have anything in common? Is there a pattern of experience that underlies all of them?

We can best answer these questions by reflecting on the biblical description of conversion and by exploring our own experience. Much has been written on the meaning of conversion, but if it does not resonate in our lives it is of little value.

The stories of personal transformation in scripture can easily leave us with the impression that conversion is a dramatic breakthrough with instantaneous results. Thus, Abraham breaks off all religious and cultural ties with the past and sets out toward an unknown land. Elisha leaves his family and his farm to become Elijah's disciple. Nathan confronts David in a moment of painful self-awareness. Simon and Andrew abandon their father and their nets to become followers of Jesus. Saul of Tarsus is struck down on the Damascus road and is transformed from a persecutor of the Way into one of its most ardent apostles.

Conversion is not always this dramatic. Nor is it necessarily instantaneous. Even in the instances which appear to be immediate and total, we can presume that there was a long struggle which led up to the moment of breakthrough. We can also presume that the struggle continues. In other words, conversion is a process—a journey in stages.

Remembering the biblical data and reflecting on personal experience, we can describe three phases in the experience of conversion: (1) a time of restless search (2) a deep inward crisis (3) a breakthrough to new life.

Conversion as Search

Lying in bed I wonder, "When will it be day?"
Rising I think, "How slowly evening comes!"
Restlessly I fret till twilight falls (Jb 7:4).

These words of Job express the endless search of the human heart for peace and fulfillment. At the center of our lives there is a hunger for something which we cannot name, a desire that we do not understand, a voice that will not be silent. We can turn to the usual distractions—our work, weekends away, television, and our friends. But these experiences cannot quiet the inner search.

We tend to view this restlessness as a sign of contradiction. We experience it as a threat, a nuisance that we hope will go away, like a headache or a cold sore. But it does not leave us easily. It haunts us like a recurring dream. It appears as an infinite void that cannot be filled.

There is a positive side to this restlessness—one

that we might overlook if we viewed life only from
its dark side. Being dissatisfied tells us that there
is more to life than we can grasp or control. It
gives us a glimpse of transcendence among the
traffic lights and rainy mornings of our lives. A
vacuum is not the same as a void. A vacuum tells
us that something is missing. It cries out for
something to fill it. In the case of the human
heart, the vacuum within us reveals a hunger not
only for something, but for Someone—for the living God.

In the story of his conversion, Thomas Merton
describes this searching spirit in his life. As a
young man of eighteen, free from school and inde-
pendent, he set out to tour Europe and to satisfy
his quest for experience. "So there I was," Merton writes in *The Seven Storey Mountain,* "with
all the liberty that I had been promising myself
for so long. The world was mine. How did I like it?
I was doing just what I pleased, and instead of being filled with happiness and well-being, I was
miserable. The love of pleasure is destined by its
very nature to defeat itself and end in frustra-
tion."

These are telling words. The earliest indication
of an experience of conversion may simply be the
feeling that all is not well in our lives. We sense
that we are out of step with the rest of humanity.
Something is out of joint. The new wine does not
rest well in old skins. We are like a camera that is
out of focus or a musical instrument that is out of
tune.

Eventually the restlessness leads us to search

for new experiences of meaning. It invites us to return to old places with new eyes. We are like Nicodemus appearing in the night to seek for truth. We are like the disciples of John following Jesus down the road and asking, "Where do you live?" We are the curious and wondering crowds that pursue Jesus across the lake, partly because we want more bread, partly because we are hungry for something we do not understand.

The early phases of conversion are like half-lost dreams. They are indistinct but persistent. They come with questions about our dogma and doubts about our lifestyle. They are filled with anger about the injustice of life and its apparent absurdity.

We grope our way in the darkness. We are aware that despite our outward bravado, we are filled with nagging fears and a sense of dread. We reach out for something more—something that has no words or shape, no voice or meaning.

Conversion as Crisis

In his book, *The Inner Eye of Love*, William Johnston describes two conditions that often accompany the experience of conversion. The first is solitude. It may be the solitude of a monastery, the quiet of a retreat, or a trek into the wilderness. What matters is that it need not be an actual experience of physical aloneness. We can touch the mystery of solitude even when we are surrounded by people. We encounter it when we are faced with a major decision about our life, our work, or our relationships. We walk in solitude when we cannot find the reasons for our restlessness or the words to express our struggle. The underlying thread in all of these experiences is a confrontation with oneself and the realization that we cannot escape into distractions or sidestep our lives.

The second catalyst to conversion is some kind of shock. It may be the death of a loved one or the sudden loss of employment. It might involve a car accident or a narrow escape from danger. Some people experience this form of crisis when they move to a new place or search for a different career. Suddenly our world falls apart. We are uprooted. The support system is gone. The mask is removed. The illusions fall away like autumn leaves and we stand naked against the sky.

These moments of painful awareness are dark and demanding, but they are also capable of transforming our lives. They may be God's way of jolting us into awareness. At the time we may only be able to describe our experience in terms of confusion and collapse. But later, when we have touched a new dimension of ourselves, we understand that something in us has been transformed and that we will never again be the same. In retrospect we recognize that at the moment when we felt most abandoned we were actually being reshaped by the power of the Spirit.

The person in crisis is not necessarily someone whose life is disintegrating. A crisis is a summons to self-reflection and purification. The external forces that seem to assault us are not the most important factor even though they are the most obvious. The real desert is the inner wasteland of our lives. There, in the wilderness of the heart, we confront the demons and darkness of our fear.

Conversion takes place only when we are faced with ultimates. Conversion is a picture of human life at the crossroads. It is Jonah, somewhere at sea on the way toward Tarshish, admitting his resistance to God and facing the storm. It is Jeremiah crying out from his depression. It is Elijah giving up in the desert and begging to die. It is Jesus in the garden. It is Peter in the cold light of dawn with the words of denial still on his tongue and the sound of the cock's crow echoing in his ears. It is Paul, blind and helpless in the dust of the Damascus road. It is any of us when we have reached the outer limits of meaning. It is any of us when we have lost our sense of direction and our self-confidence. In that midnight moment there is a promise and a hint of light. It is a promise about darkness becoming dawn and of death being transformed into life.

Conversion as Breakthrough

At what point does an apparent collapse become a breakthrough to life? How do we find the narrow door that leads to new growth?

The breakthrough to life occurs at the moment in which we let go of our desire to control our lives and instead entrust them into the hands of God. This requires a painful leap of faith. At a time of inner crisis we would rather not face the implications of radical change. We store up our defenses and prepare for battle. And as our illusions begin to collapse, we scramble to maintain the status quo or look for a place to hide. Ironically, we often find ourselves struggling against the very people and forces that could make us whole. What can we do to transform our struggle against life into a journey toward life?

Jesus answered this question by setting a young child in front of his disciples and telling them: "I tell you solemnly, unless you change and become like little children you will never enter into the kingdom of heaven" (Mt 18:3). Children live in a spirit of wonder. They are open to surprises and willing to take risks. They know that they are dependent on someone else for their life and safety.

A childlike attitude is the key to conversion. Before conversion is anything else, it is a breakthrough to trust, a willingness to let go of our fears and our defenses. At the moment in which we are willing to risk everything for the kingdom, we break through to eternal life. Like the prodigal son, we suddenly "come to our senses." We turn and begin the long journey home.

For some people this final breakthrough is dramatic and moving. When Thomas Merton finally made the decision to become a Catholic it came with a suddenness that even he could not understand. He had been reading one afternoon when he was seized with an irresistible urge to leave everything immediately and go seek out a Catholic priest. As he walked in the rain his whole life seemed to come together: "Everything inside of me began to sing—to sing with peace, to sing with strength and to sing with conviction."

For others the final decision is quiet and deep. Cardinal Newman describes his final conversion in these words: "I was not conscious to myself, on my conversion, of any change, intellectual or moral, wrought in my mind . . . but it was like coming into port after a rough sea."

Conversion: Coming Down to Earth

The gospels abound with stories about conversion and the people who experience this gift from God. One of the most heart-warming of these stories involves a man named Zaccheus, who, in his honest search for life, ends up being transformed by the Lord. Zaccheus belonged to a group of businessmen who made their living by collecting taxes for one of the great financial companies of Rome. The encounter which he has with Jesus is one of the most striking stories of conversion in the gospels.

Except for his wealth and the fact that he was a senior tax collector, Zaccheus had very little going for him. Because of his profession he was despised by his fellow Jews and looked down upon as a sinner. He was short of stature and probably not physically attractive. In addition to all this, he had a reputation, like most publicans, for being dishonest in his business dealings.

In Aramaic the name Zaccheus means "the pure or innocent one." Given Zaccheus' way of life and his reputation, there is obviously a note of irony in his name. On the other hand, perhaps Zaccheus is well-named. Whatever his background and methods, he is clearly a seeker of truth. He would have had every reason to shun the crowds and seek security in his riches.

But something was stirring in him—a hunger of the heart and a restlessness of the spirit that would not be silent. Imagine a wealthy man climbing a sycamore tree to catch a glimpse of the itinerant teacher from Nazareth! There must have been a sparkle in the Rabbi's eyes when he stopped under the sycamore and peered up into its branches.

Jesus saw something that the rest of the crowd did not see. He looked beyond the social labels and the externals to see the heart of a man who was seeking for life. Jesus saw the true Zaccheus—the playful child who longed to throw off the weight of his past and to be born again.

Come down, Zaccheus. Come down to earth. Come back to community. You are loved, forgiven, and accepted. You are a changed man. You are Zaccheus—innocent and pure of heart.

The breakthrough to life came to Zaccheus like an overflowing energy that had waited too long to be shared. "Look, Lord," he proclaimed, "I am going to give half my property to the poor, and if I have cheated anybody I will pay him back four times the amount" (Lk 19:8).

Conversion is a transformation of life. It presupposes that we are willing to search for a new perspective. It implies that we, like Zaccheus, are willing to climb trees to find God and come back down to earth with new hearts.

CHAPTER FIVE

Setting Out

"Once the hand is laid to the plow, no one who looks back is fit for the kingdom of God."

—Luke 9:62

IT was time to go. We had finished breakfast and lingered over our coffee. We had carried out the last boxes of books and tied down the trunk of the car. The sun slanted through the trees and glistened on the dew. The morning spoke of summer and unfinished journeys.

It was time to go. My father knew it and was silent. My mother knew it and was solicitous. No one knew it better than I. Only two weeks before, I had been ordained a priest.

The next day my family and friends gathered at the parish church to celebrate a mass of thanksgiving. There was laughter and song and tears of joy. There were old friends and classmates and a flood of affirmation. But the celebration was over now. Today I was leaving for my first assignment. I was suddenly and deeply afraid. It wasn't leaving home that frightened me. I had been doing that with regularity during the long years of seminary education.

But today was different. I wasn't just leaving home in a definitive manner. I was setting out on my life's work. All of the years of preparation were coming to a turning point in this moment. A decision was about to be tested. A vision was about to take flesh. A call was to become a mission.

I felt the clarity of the moment in the churning of my stomach and the tightness in my shoulders. Doubts welled up in me. The ancient dread of failure. The grip of uncertainty. The flood of questions. What if I fail? What if I can't bear the pressures of parish ministry? What if I can't measure up to the responsibility? What if the whole thing is an absurd mistake?

I went for one last tour of the orchard and stood at the brow of the hill. The alfalfa was in blossom and ready for the first cutting. The fields basked under the bright sun. I thought of the summers I had spent close to this earth, touching its mystery and moving with the rhythm of its life.

I returned to the house and stood for a moment in the doorway of the kitchen—that crossroad of life where the family gathered for food and laughter and tears. There was nowhere to turn now—nowhere except toward the car and the road that led toward the river and the highway. I had walked back through the familiar surroundings. I had recollected my life. I had gathered my freedom. I had faced my fears.

It was time to go. I moved quickly toward the ritual of goodbye. The words flowed from a long tradition of farewells: We'll see you soon. Take care. Don't work too hard. I'll call. There were smiles and tears and embraces. And then the road.

I drove the two hour trip along the route which I had taken so many times while I was in the seminary. The road was the same. The landmarks were as familiar as old friends. The river moved south with me as always. But something was different this time. Something had changed. I felt uprooted and alone. The terrain toward which I was driving loomed before me as an unknown land. I smiled to myself. I was doing this, I thought, with far less trust than Abraham, the father of believers, but I was doing it all the same. In the face of my fears I felt a surge of freedom, the sense that I had taken my life in my hands and ventured forth toward the future with anxious but clear eyes.

Setting Out

The feelings which surrounded the departure for my first assignment are by no means limited to me or to ministry. There are moments in everyone's life when they experience the full burden of their choices and the questions and fears which flow from freedom. There are times of clarity in every person's pilgrimage—times when we must face the full consequences of our decisions.

Whatever the circumstances, we recognize in

these moments that something essential is at stake—something within us which will stand or fall. In these crucial moments we come face to face with the holy. We experience what Rudolph Otto describes as the *"mysterium tremendens et fascinans"*—the mystery that is both frightening and attracting. Somehow we know that our lives and our integrity depend on the way in which we carry out our decisions. There is a sense that this counts, that life is and will be different because of the manner of our hearts and the attitude of our freedom.

In scripture this key moment of freedom is often associated with a *setting out.* It may involve an actual physical movement toward a new location. Or it may be a journey of the heart toward a new world of interiority. What matters most is that it is a breakthrough of the spirit, a leap of freedom, a peak experience of human responsibility.

Setting out is the road that leads beyond conversion. Conversion is the transforming experience; setting out is what follows. When we set out we choose to face the implications of our new stage of growth. We walk the road which has opened up before us. We put our hand to the plow and, at least for the moment, we do not look back.

"The journey of a thousand miles begins beneath your feet," says the old proverb. The ground beneath our feet—it is there, in the commonplace and the everyday, in the soil of joys and sorrows, that our vision is tested and purified. It is in the first step, the first mile, the initial leap that we shape and define the road that lies ahead.

Adsum: I Am Ready

Before the recent updating of sacramental rites, the Latin form of ordination contained at least one powerful gesture. It took place at the beginning of the ceremony of ordination. The candidates stood before the ordaining prelate. There was a moment of silence. Then the bishop called out the name of each candidate. When the individual's name was called, he responded in a clear and loud voice: *"Adsum."* Then he took one step forward.

Adsum can be translated in many different ways, none of which adequately expresses the meaning of the original Latin. It can be translated as "I am here," or simply, "here" or "present," as though one were responding to a roll call in a classroom. In the context of ordination this is clearly an inadequate understanding of this solemn moment. The bishop is not taking roll call. He is, on behalf of the entire community of believers, calling candidates to sacred orders. He is calling them to make a free decision of life, the most fundamental choice of their human journey.

As in the ancient biblical experience, this is not a general call to a group, but an individual call to this person at this time in sacred history. It is an invitation to respond out of the depth of one's freedom to the call of God and the community. The response to such a call is not a passive ac-

knowledgment that one is "present and account-
ed for," a mere admission that one is physically
located in this juncture of space and time. To say
Adsum is to respond with one's total freedom
after long and careful preparation. It means to be
ready. It declares that one is prepared for the consequences. *Adsum* literally means that "I am
towards." I am reaching out to the future. I offer
my life and give my energy. I am attentive and
listening, walking, near at hand to the flow of the
Spirit.

Adsum is another word for setting out toward
God. It expresses the sense of poised freedom in
the heart of a disciple. It is the leap of the heart
and the flight of the Spirit.

Here I Am, Send Me

Adsum is the inward yes of those who trust
God's way enough to follow him into darkness.
When God tested Abraham's love for Isaac he
called out to the patriarch, "Abraham, Abraham!" "Ready!" he replied (Gn 22:1). When God
called his people out of Egypt he told them to eat
the passover meal with sandals on their feet and
staff in hand—ready for the journey (Ex 12:11).
When young Samuel was awakened for the third
time in the night by the voice of Yahweh calling
out his name, he responded, "Speak, Lord, for
your servant is listening" (I Sm 3:11). The prophet Isaiah described his call in these words: "I
heard the voice of the Lord saying, 'Whom shall I
send? Who will be our messenger?' I answered,
'Here I am, send me'" (Is 6:8-9).

When the angel Gabriel came to Mary with the invitation to be the mother of the messiah, she hesitated only long enough to make clear the implications of her response. Then she answered: "I am the handmaid of the Lord. Let it be done to me according to your word" (Lk 1:38).

Finally, the author of Hebrews attributes to Jesus the words of Psalm 40: "Then I said, just as I was commanded in the scroll of the book, 'God, here I am! I am coming to do your will'" (He 10:7).

What do Abraham, Samuel, Isaiah, Mary, and Jesus and every believer have in common? They stand before God with a decisive spirit. At the turning points of their lives they were willing to say *"Adsum!"* I am ready. Speak, Lord, your servant is listening. Here I am, send me. Let it be done to me according to your will.

Setting Out: An Act of Faith

Is there anything inherent in the experience of setting out that makes it an act of faith? Leaving the security of the present to brave the future appears to be a natural part of the rhythm of life. We see it in the young robin who is nudged from its nest by a watchful mother to begin its first solo flight. We see it in the first halting steps of a child. Setting out seems to be as natural as the restless urge of adventure which drives the human spirit beyond borders to new frontiers.

Adventuring is instinctive to life. Why speak of it as an act of faith? What transforms instinct into grace? Where does faith inform freedom to make our journey one that is done with God?

Clearly the answer to these questions is not related to the external appearance of the human pilgrimage. There have been many journeys which required great courage but not necessarily faith. One can launch a rocket to the moon and not believe in God. We must look inward to discover faith's role in the human adventure. Faith focuses on the interior attitude rather than the external circumstances. Setting out becomes an act of faith when we approach the basic choices of our lives as a response to a call from God. Setting out becomes a way of sharing in the paschal mystery when we understand our lives as patterned after the journey of Jesus. Faith transforms our setting out into an encounter with God.

The life of Saul of Tarsus is a clear example of the difference which faith makes in interpreting our choices. Saul's experience on the road to Damascus was more than a shattering event of consciousness. It was an encounter with the risen Christ. "Who are you, Lord?" Saul asked in astonishment. This question was to remain with Paul for the rest of his life. Long after he had been led blind and helpless into Damascus; long after Ananias had laid hands on him; long after he had set out to preach the gospel, this question would continue to shape and form his life. Who are you, Lord? What do you ask of my life? Where are you calling me to go? What is the road that I am to walk?

Faith makes every setting out a response to the living God. Faith transforms the mythic journey of the hero into the real life experience of taking responsibility for our lives and our freedom.

Setting Out: An Act of Freedom

"Not I, not I, but the wind that blows through me!" This is the opening line of D. H. Lawrence's poem, "Song of a Man Who Has Come Through." Anyone who has survived a time of crisis or who has experienced a breakthrough to life knows that there is an energy within us that is greater than what we can claim as our own. Some call this adrenalin or true grit. Others speak of instinct or psychic forces. As Christians we reach further into mystery and claim that it is the Spirit who stirs in us. Not I, not I, but the Spirit who blows in me.

"Where the Spirit of the Lord is, there is freedom" (II Cor 3:17). This is Paul's way of telling us that it is the Spirit who enables us to put our commitments into action. The Spirit is the divine energy that stretches us beyond our reach to do the will of the Father.

This perspective on Christian liberty is far different from the popular notions of freedom which permeate our contemporary world. It is safe to assume that the average person does not see any significant relationship between feeedom and commitment. On the contrary, freedom in today's society is often equated with a lack of decisiveness. It means "keeping your options open" and refusing to be limited by clear choices. The liberated person is pictured as the one who is not tied down by the responsibilities of roles or structures or personal relationships.

In the Word of God, by way of contrast, freedom can only be achieved through commitment. We become free only when we give direction to our unshaped lives. Discipleship is training in freedom. It focuses our energy and gives substance to our vision. Until we have made a commitment we have not yet realized the true energy of the human heart. We have not yet touched the power to give ourselves away in love. To know this energy is to encounter God and his grace.

The Sound of Trees, the Call of the Heart

Setting out is the act of putting our lives into action. It is the way in which the Word takes flesh in our lives. It is the act of choosing to write our own story without knowing the script. Setting out is our way of knowing the truth about ourselves—a truth no longer confined to daydreams, but a truth of action and commitment, a truth that sets us free for life.

When we put our choices into action we go beyond the cycles of nature and their predictable patterns. We lay claim to what is uniquely ours—the gift of our humanity, the burden of being free to follow the Spirit. In his poem, "The Sound of the Trees," Robert Frost describes this tension between the inevitable rhythms of nature and the decisiveness of the human heart. In the night wind the trees speak of making the long journey toward dawn. But they are not going anywhere. Trees, like the rest of nature, are part of the earth's constant cycle. "They are that that talks of going/But never gets away." As he listens to the sound of the trees, the poet touches the urgency of his own life:

> *I shall set forth for somewhere,*
> *I shall make the reckless choice*
> *Some day when they are in voice*
> *And tossing so as to scare*
> *The white clouds over them on.*
> *I shall have less to say,*
> *But I shall be gone.*

He Who Puts His Hand To the Plow

It is not often that we have the singleness of purpose to act decisively. Our vision tends to be clouded. Our choices are tentative and conditional. Even at the moments of great decisions our hearts are often distracted and divided. We lack purity of heart, which Kierkegaard defines as "the ability to will one thing." We walk forward while glancing over our shoulder and wondering if there was a different road that we should have taken.

On occasion, however, we do attain moments of authentic integration. These are the graced moments when we gather our lives in full awareness of the options and unknown circumstances. We choose freely. We decide upon the road we will walk. And at least for a time, we do not look backward in regret. We walk toward the future with hope.

Jesus asked his disciples to follow him with this

kind of decisive spirit. He asked them to make clear commitments. One day someone came to Jesus and said, "I will follow you, Lord, but first let me go and say goodbye to my people at home." Jesus turned to the man and said, "Once the hand is laid to the plow, no one who looks back is fit for the kingdom of God" (Lk 9:61-62).

What did Jesus mean? Was he advocating an insensitive attitude toward families and friends? Was he saying that we can never look back and wonder if we chose the right road? Obviously not. In the prophetic and Jewish style of hyperbole Jesus is proclaiming that the gospel is not peripheral. It is central. The kingdom has priority over everything else. It demands a radical decision that cannot be compromised even by the most pressing things.

The Decisive Moment

Perhaps we can better understand Jesus' challenging words to the prospective disciple in Luke's gospel, if we look more carefully at the scriptural background.

As a Jewish Rabbi, Jesus would have been well acquainted with the Hebrew scriptures. They were the foundation of his prayer life and of his teaching. Commentators tell us that Jesus' response on this occasion may well have been a reference to the following passage in the First Book of Kings:

> *"Leaving there, he came on Elisha son of Shaphat as he was plowing behind twelve yoke of oxen, he himself being with the twelfth. Elijah passed near to him and*

threw his cloak over him. Elisha left his oxen and ran after Elijah. 'Let me kiss my father and mother, then I will follow you' he said. Elijah answered, "Go, go back; for have I done anything to you?" Elisha turned away, took the pair of oxen and slaughtered them. He used the plow for cooking the oxen, then gave to his men who ate. He then rose, and followed Elijah and became his servant."

—I Kgs 19:19-21

Elijah was getting old. Or perhaps just weary of being the "troubler of Israel" (cf I Kgs 18:17). He knew that his mission was not completed. He also knew that there was not time enough for him to finish his work. The task was too great. The people of Israel were too slow to understand and too stubborn to change. On Mount Horeb, Yahweh told Elijah to seek out Elisha, son of Shaphat, and anoint him as disciple and successor.

Thus, the focus of the drama shifts to Elisha. Who was he? Why did God choose him to be the successor of one of Israel's most fearsome prophets? We know only a few bare facts about Elisha. But they are significant pieces of information which help us to understand the turning point of Elisha's life.

Elisha was the son of a very rich farmer. At the time that he was called he was out in his father's fields plowing with twelve yoke of oxen. Elijah approached Elisha in silence. He put his cloak over the younger man as he was following the last team of oxen. This quiet gesture bore a striking message which Elisha immediately understood.

In the ancient Hebrew world a man's cloak was one of his most valued possessions. It was his shelter from the burning sun, his protection against the storm and the cold of the night. The cloak symbolized the person himself with his power and presence. When Elijah placed his cloak on the shoulders of Elisha he was saying in effect that he wanted to share his life, his call, and his mission with his future successor.

There is a further meaning in Elijah's dramatic gesture. In biblical times, when a man placed his cloak over another person, it symbolized a claim of ownership. Elijah was not only offering to share his power and mission with Elisha, he was actually laying claim, in God's name, to Elisha's life. It was a clear call to discipleship.

Elisha understood this with a clarity that surprised even Elijah. Elisha immediately ran after the older prophet and told him that he needed only enough time to say goodbye to his parents at home. Then he would follow him. Elijah's response has a note of irony about it. He appears to make light of the gesture which he had performed. Perhaps he wanted to give Elisha more time to think. But the Spirit was stirring in Elisha's heart. He knew that time had run out. He had spent long hours thinking about his life. For months and years he had turned the earth into furrows and gazed at the sky. Even then he knew that the call would eventually come. It was only a matter of time. And today time had run out for Elisha. There were no more hours to reflect, no more time to hesitate—not even time to go home and say goodbye. This was the decisive moment. This was the time of setting out.

With clarity of mind and decisiveness of heart, Elisha broke up his plow and built a fire with it. He slaughtered two of the oxen and barbecued them for his hired men. Then, after a hasty farewell picnic, he left everything to follow Elijah.

Elisha's life is a striking example of what it means to set out on a mission. When God's call came into his life, he understood it to be a decisive claim on his attention. The kingdom breaks into our lives with the same urgency. It comes with a power that is irresistible and compelling. We must recognize the call when it comes. There will be time enough for struggle and growth. Time enough for questions and doubts. We have been preparing for this moment for our entire lives. This is the time of response, the hour of decision.

The call of Elisha provides a new perspective on Jesus' enigmatic words in the gospel of Luke. When one of his followers asked permission to bid farewell to his family, Jesus told him: "Once the hand is laid to the plow, no one who looks back is fit for the kingdom of God." There is good reason to believe that Jesus has the story of Elisha in mind when he gave this response. Elisha was a model of decisiveness. Once he decided to put his hand to the plow of prophecy, he no longer looked back toward his father's house or his father's fields. He had heard the call. He had found the treasure. He set out in search of God.

CHAPTER SIX

Following

"If anyone wants to be a follower of mine, let him renounce himself and take up his cross and follow me. For anyone who wants to save his life will lose it; but anyone who loses his life for my sake, and for the sake of the gospel, will save it."

—Mark 8:34–35

IT was only an hour past midnight when the young Rabbi left the house and walked beyond the village streets toward the edge of the desert. He moved past twisted olive trees, crossed a rocky plateau, and climbed toward the summit of a hill. For a few minutes he looked toward the east where the desert stretched out in the moonlight as far as the eye could see.

Then, still facing the direction of the dawn, he sat down on a rock. His body became motionless in prayer. A stillness came over him that seemed more expansive than the night. It was as though he were in touch with something deep within him. He remained this way until the first streaks of light began to shoot upwards across the sky.

The sun was well risen when his friends came climbing up the rocky ledge in search of him.

"Everybody is looking for you," Simon said. His voice was edged with impatience. The Rabbi looked at him for a few moments in silence. When he responded his voice was quiet and confident. "Then let us go elsewhere," he said, "to the neighboring towns so that I can preach there too, because that is why I came" (Mk 1:37–38).

Everybody Is Looking

I have long been fascinated with this brief portrait of Jesus. It reveals a dimension of his personality that we often neglect. It is a profile of Jesus in search of personal space. It speaks of a man who longs so deeply to pray that he goes forth in the night watch.

What did Jesus find in the desert? What presence permeated him? What did he experience in those long hours before dawn? More than that, what was so powerful and attractive in him that it drew others to seek him out and to follow him?

Everybody is looking for you. There is a note of irony in Simon's words. Perhaps it would have been more correct to say that everybody is *looking*—looking for an elusive happiness that is always beyond their reach; looking for enough food to fill their stomachs, enough security to give them peace, enough love to give them a sense of belonging, enough hope to keep on walking.

Everybody is looking. Looking for someone to trust in, looking for a vision to walk by, a reason to live, and a reason to die. Even when they cannot find words for it, everyone is seeking for fulfillment and for the secret that lies within them.

Everybody Is Looking for You

There may be irony in Simon's statement, but there is also a declaration. This deeper truth of the gospel must still be reckoned with. The secret of Christianity is that, in the end, it *is* Jesus that the crowds are seeking. He is the way, the truth, the life. He is lamb of God and shepherd of the flock. He is gate and doorway. He is bread of life and cup of salvation. He is the vine and the dwelling place of love. He is morning star and rising dawn, the first born of many brothers and sisters, the suffering servant. Or, as the early Christian community declared, Jesus is Lord.

In the world of mystery and in the desert of faith Simon's words ring true. Everybody *is* looking for Jesus. The crowds are stunned by this man. The hungry come to him for food; the sinners for forgiveness; the blind for sight; the curious for wonders; the seeking for answers; the disciples for reassurance.

Everybody is looking for Jesus. They have few words for what they feel and no way of expressing the ache within or the restlessness of their lives. But there are signs that point to the hunger that haunts them. There is a weariness behind their eyes and a longing in their hearts. They may not be able to find the words or the gestures to say it, but it is the Lord whom they seek.

A Society of Seekers

Technologically our society appears to be a long way from the Palestinian world of the first century A.D. But it carries the same thirst, the same hunger, the same ache and restlessness. We can look at our society and echo the words of Simon. Everybody is looking—and looking all the more as they claim to have found the answer or to have opened up the door to fulfillment.

Today's crowds are looking in ways and in places that are as desperate as they are direct, as superficial as they are sophisticated. They seek for meaning in eastern meditation or in going back to nature. They look for significance in sexual experimentation, bio-medical feedback, chemical dependency. They look for life in the quest for riches and the search for fame, in cults, self-therapy, and natural foods.

In the midst of all this the figure of Jesus challenges us to reach beyond the surface of our lives in search of a deeper truth. In the 60s many intellectuals claimed that God was dead. Some social scientists declared that religion was a culturally acceptable but irrelevant part of the human psyche, a security blanket for ignorance. Therapy, they said, can take the place of religion. Science can create a brave new world.

But secularity is in the process of discovering its own dark limitations. Vietnam, political scandals, oil spills, oil shortages, and the experience at Three Mile Island have all cast some doubt across the brave new world. The experience of God is changing. The mainline churches are in trouble.

However, Christianity is not dying. The question of Jesus is still with us. His meaning may be misunderstood, exploited, and challenged, but it is not forgotten. He is the haunting figure that will not leave us. Jesus is the question that will not go away. He is the presence of possibility in a world of human despair.

From Seeker to Disciple

Many in our contemporary culture have made seeking a way of life. They move from one psychic or emotional trip to the next with the ease of changing fashions or hair styles. There are almost as many cultural fads today as there are groups of people who declare themselves to be relevant. In his film, *Manhattan*, Woody Allen portrays a disillusioned script writer who abandons popular T.V. programming to write an honest novel about contemporary culture. At one point he describes his ex-wife in these terms: "She was a kindergarten teacher, then she got into drugs and moved to San Francisco. She went to est, became a moonie. She works for the William Morris agency now."

Whether such a personal odessey is a sign of cultural deterioration or simply the outcome of a restless age, one thing is clear. Our age lacks a clear vision. In the end the fads become distractions from authentic human commitment, a way of escaping the dark questions about personal integrity and the moral quality of our lives. There is a general lack of commitment—in relationships, in art, in politics, in lifestyles. Even where there is a genuine questioning, it is often accompanied by the assumption that the answers must be comfortable and well suited to a consumerist society.

Clearly there is a need to move beyond the surface. There is a lingering demand for honesty and a willingness to face our illusions. Perhaps we can still clarify our vision and follow it with a decisive spirit. To find a vision and to follow it—this may well be the pressing issue of our age.

The religious term for following the truth of our lives is *discipleship*. One who is looking is called a seeker. One who decides upon a way and pursues it is called a disciple. Disciples do not cease to be seekers, but when seekers choose to become disciples, they make a decision to attach themselves to this way of life, this vision, this road. A disciple is one who is willing to take on the implications of a vision.

Discipleship is what happens when curiosity is transformed into conversion, and conversion, in turn, becomes a way of life. Discipleship is the spiritual journey of following the vision and of being faithful to a way of life. It is what one does along the road after one has set out for the future. The word disciple means a learner—one who is pursuing the truth with openness and dedication. It implies that one is in the process of integrating values into experience and sharing them with others.

Discipleship implies an inner pilgrimage which consumes one's being and which makes radical demands on one's life. Hence it also conveys the dimension of *discipline*. Discipline is not an arbitrary harshness imposed on life from the outside. It is the form through which commitment ex-

presses itself. Commitment is another word for
the cost of discipleship.

Levels of Discipleship

During his public ministry Jesus attracted
widespread attention in Judea and Galilee.
Crowds followed after him. Individuals sought
him out. Friends accompanied him. It is clear in
reading the gospel accounts that everyone did not
follow Jesus for the same reasons. Christian discipleship is the call to enter into a personal relationship with Jesus. Such a relationship admits of
degrees of distance or intimacy. Like every other
process of growth, being a disciple involves differing levels of commitment.

In his book, *Discipleship and Priesthood,* Karl
Schelke outlines three stages of growth in following Christ. They might be described as three levels of "coming to" Jesus. *Kommen* is a German
word which means "to come toward" or "to follow." Schelke describes the three levels of discipleship as (1) *zukommen*—to approach someone
primarily out of curiosity; (2) *mitkommen*—to
come to someone out of need or to accompany
someone in a project or concern; (3)
nachkommen—to make a total commitment to a
person together with the radical decision to accept the consequences of such a relationship.

These three levels of discipleship furnish us
with a useful model for understanding the response of various people to Jesus in the gospels.
They also provide us with a basis for reflecting on

the meaning of our own call to Christian discipleship.

The Crowds and the Curious: Following
at a Distance

Many people came after Jesus because of his
reputation as a wonder-worker. They simply
wanted to find out if the rumors were true about
the rabbi. They came hoping to see miracles or to
witness unusual events.

Who are these "distant disciples?" They are the
crowds that followed Jesus around the Sea of
Galilee in search of more bread. They are the sick
and the lame, the blind and the lepers, the possessed and the outcast, who would follow after
any wonder-worker who promised to heal them.

The scribes and the Pharisees were also distant
observers of Jesus. They saw him as a religious re-
bel, a fanatic who represented a significant danger to the established religious order. When they
came to him it was only to entrap him in his
speech or to look for evidence to destroy him.

What do these various groups and individuals
have in common? They are all curious about Jesus
for reasons of exploitation or self-interest. They
have no particular commitment toward him as a
person or toward his vision. They are not interested in his message or his way of life.

"The crowd," writes Kierkegaard, "is untruth."
The crowd does not come out of conviction but only out of curiosity. They have no investment except for their own needs or political interests.

That is why they can just as easily be moved toward rejection as they can be led to acceptance. Mostly they are moved by convention and the mood of the moment. Individually, many of them may even have assumed the title of disciple. Individually, they may be respectable citizens. But they are detached followers. They are disciples without depth.

The Interested and the Invited: Following with a Willing Spirit

Not all of those who approached Jesus out of need did so for selfish or exploitive reasons. Many of the sick came to him with genuine faith. Matthew recounts the story of two blind men who were following Jesus down the street begging for healing. Jesus turned to them and said: "Do you believe I can do this?" They said, 'Sir, we do.' Then Jesus touched their eyes saying 'Your faith deserves it, so let this be done for you'" (Mt 9: 27–31).

Jesus saw that these men brought more than their blindness to him. He saw more than need in their eyes. He recognized that they were also open to a relationship. He knew that they were seeking to become whole not only physically but also spiritually and emotionally.

Jesus did not come primarily to work miracles, nor did he heal indiscriminately. He responded to the presence of faith and called people into relationship with him. "Your faith has made you whole." These are frequent words in Jesus' encounters with the blind and the lame. Their faith was a significant step beyond curiosity or self-interest. It was a leap into relationship. It was the beginning of true discipleship.

There were other seekers who came to Jesus in the quest for truth and understanding. The two disciples of John the Baptist followed him down the road. When Jesus turned and asked them what they wanted, they replied, "Rabbi, where do you live?" (Jn 1:35-39). The consequences were not yet clear for them. They did not know clearly what it was they were seeking.

But they did know that they wanted to spend time with Jesus. They wanted somehow to be a part of his life. In this group we can also picture Nicodemus and the woman at the well. We can recall the young scribe who promised to follow Jesus wherever he would go, and the rich young man who came seeking eternal life (Mt 19:16).

Still others in the gospel followed Jesus neither out of physical need nor because of an intellectual quest. They came after him because they had been invited by Jesus—singled out and challenged to leave the past behind and to begin a new life. This includes all of the disciples in their initial response to Jesus' call—Peter and Andrew leaving their nets, Levi abandoning his tax collector's stand, Simon turning aside from political aspirations. It includes the women who accompanied Jesus and shared his ministry. Martha, Mary and Lazarus are there too, together with Mary Magdalene and the others who had experienced his compassion and strength in their lives.

What do these have in common? They have all

made an initial step toward faith and discipleship. Each of them has decided to follow Jesus in some initial way. Their faith and fidelity still has to be tested. Their willingness to pay the cost of discipleship has not yet been proven. They possess a willing spirit and a seeking heart.

In some instances there is even enthusiasm and confidence. But it is a vision that does not burn with intensity, a cross not yet taken up, a word not yet made flesh, a promise without performance, a relationship that has not been stretched by time or pain or even failure.

Disciples and Witnesses: Following as Total Commitment

"He who is not with me is against me; he who does not gather with me scatters" (Lk 11:23). Jesus spoke these words at the turning point of his ministry. He realized with a heavy heart and a prophet's realism that, humanly speaking, his mission would fail. For months his words had fallen on deaf ears. His miracles were misunderstood, his relationships misconstrued. The crowds clamored for more signs. The Zealots demanded revolution. The Pharisees and scribes sought to trap him. Even his own followers were confused about the implications of his teaching and the demands of discipleship.

Jesus knew the road that he must walk and he chose to follow it freely. But his awareness of the role of suffering in his life also had implications for those who followed him. It was the hour of Jesus, but it was also the hour of his followers. This was the time of decision, the hour of testing, the moment to face the implications of disciple-ship.

The first to be confronted with these implications were the crowds. When they continued to seek him after the multiplication of the loaves, Jesus confronted them: "I tell you most solemnly you are not looking for me because you have seen the signs but because you had all the bread you wanted to eat. Do not work for food that cannot last, but work for food that endures to eternal life" (Jn 6:26).

When Jesus told the crowds that he was the true bread of life and that they must eat his body and drink his blood, it was too much for them to accept. They turned aside. "After this," writes John, "many of his disciples left him and stopped going with him" (Jn 6:60).

The test of a disciple is his or her willingness to follow in the footsteps of the master. As Jesus moved toward his darkest hour of self-giving, his relationships narrowed dramatically. The crowds changed their minds. Nicodemus was not heard from again. The young scribe lost his enthusiasm. And before dawn Simon Peter had denied that he ever knew this rabbi from Nazareth.

The response to such testing need not be des-pair. The road to discipleship leads not only to the cross and suffering, but also to a confrontation with our own fears, our confusion, and even our denial and our failure. The true disciple of Jesus is one who is willing to pass through even personal failure in order to die with the Lord and find his healing.

Peter and the other disciples failed at the time

of testing, but they turned back to Jesus and clung to his love and compassion. This became the most important turning point in their relationship with Jesus. It was to be their breakthrough to authentic discipleship.

It was a long way from the shores of the Sea of Galilee to the morning of Pentecost. It was a long road from the initial enthusiasm to the final breakthrough to total commitment. Jesus understood and accepted this painful process of growth in his disciples. Even at the darkest moment when he realized that those closest to him would abandon him, he reached out to them in compassion and care.

It happened as Jesus had prayed it would. In the power of the Spirit a frightened group of people became true apostles. Those who had scattered in the night now stood out in the light. And, in a few short years after the resurrection of the Lord, they gave their lives for the good news. They became disciples and witnesses of new life.

A Different Kind of Discipleship

How can we understand the deeper implications of Christian discipleship? What is distinctive about following Jesus?

In order to answer these questions we must look briefly at the relationship which existed between Jewish teachers and their disciples in the first century of the Christian era. Only then will we be able to understand how radically Jesus changed the nature of this relationship.

After the Israelites returned from exile, the

Law became the primary object of their religious teaching and experience. The masters who were responsible for preserving the purity of the Torah were referred to as "doctors of the Law."

At the time that Jesus began his public ministry there were many different approaches to the Law. They varied according to their interpretation of certain practices and doctrines. They were also influenced by differing political ideals. But all of the schools had one thing in common: they looked upon the teacher as the master and the students as servants. In Hebrew the word "rabbi" literally means "my master."

For the most part, the rabbis settled in one geographical area. They could be found teaching in the schools or at the gate of the town. The students, most of whom were the socially elite, were expected to seek out the Rabbi whom they wished to choose as master. There was very little involvement between the rabbi and his disciples.

In both his message and in his style of teaching Jesus stands apart from the other rabbis of his time. In the first place, Jesus decided to become an itinerant rabbi in order to carry the message of the kingdom to the poor and the outcast.

Jesus took his experience of the good news to the common people who could not afford to pay for instruction at the rabbinical centers. His style of teaching was also different from the others. Jesus did not belong to a school or to any of the accepted juridical categories of interpretation. He spoke from his own vision and from his experience of the Father in his life.

The most striking difference between Jesus and the other rabbis, however, is the relationship which Jesus establishes with his disciples. For Jesus a disciple is not simply someone who learns doctrines or theories. It is a person who shares a deep relationship with him.

Jesus does not just teach theory or interpret the law. He unveils his deepest self to those who follow him. Jesus changes this hierarchical model. "I no longer call you servants," he tells his followers, "I call you friends, because I have made known everything I have learned from my Father."

To be a disciple of Jesus is to go beyond learning to love, beyond curiosity to commitment. It is no longer just a question of keeping the Torah. The disciples are not bound to a doctrine but to a person.

Torah means "law" or "way of living." Jesus asks his disciples to do more than keep the law. He invites them to become united with him in a personal relationship of love and mutual trust. Jesus *is* the Torah. He is the way that leads toward truth, the eternal Word become flesh. Discipleship takes us beyond the pursuit of truth or the search for a meaningful way of life.

The distinctive quality of Christian discipleship is the total commitment that it demands to the person of Jesus and the willingness to integrate his life into our own.

CHAPTER SEVEN

Growing

"May he give you the power through his Spirit for your hidden self to grow strong. . ."
—Ephesians 3:16

ONE April afternoon when I was in the seventh grade and the earth was stirring with spring, I went out to plant trees. I was only thirteen years old then—young enough to be a boy, but old enough to think about the future and where it would take me. I had taken on a forestry project that year which required that I collect and identify the various species of trees in our area. Part of the project also involved planting new trees.

The earth smelled moist and rich as I turned it over with the spade. The sunlight felt warm and reassuring. It was the perfect time for planting. I placed each of the Norway spruce seedlings in the ground and carefully covered their roots with fresh earth. Then I poured extra water on them to help them take root.

When I was finished I took a few minutes to rest and to survey the new seedlings. They were only a few inches tall—so tiny and fragile that it was difficult for me to imagine that someday they would grow into trees.

Almost thirty years have come and gone since that April afternoon. The tiny seedlings moved through the seasons quietly and consistently. I watched them grow from tiny saplings into hearty young firs, and, almost without my realizing it, into mature trees, beyond my height and beyond my reach. Now their branches sway gently in the August breeze and bend with snow after a January storm.

If I had it to do all over again, I would plant more trees. I've learned something from them about what it means to grow. They are markers along life's journey, companions in the unfolding of the human story. Their growth is not unlike our own. They do not reach maturity in one growing season. Their life unfolds in cyclic patterns of years and decades.

Each season has its own experience of growth, its own time and moment, its own path toward life. Trees know the sudden flowering of spring and the long wait of winter. They stand as tall in the midnight darkness as they do in the noonday sun. They remind us that growth is not a phenomenon of youth but a life-long process of unfolding and deepening. They speak to us of continuity and of roots that cannot be measured or seen.

On occasion I still go back to the spruce trees I planted that April afternoon. I go back to listen, to think, and to pray. I find myself thinking of Paul's words to his friends at Corinth: "I did the planting, Apollos did the watering, but God made

things grow. Neither the planter nor the waterer matters: only God, who makes things grow" (I Cor 2:6-7).

All in Good Time

It is not easy for us to respect the flow of time. In our age, science has gone beyond the usual limitations of time to make the present moment available with new immediacy. We can transcend the barriers of time through commercial jet travel, through radio and television, and satellite communication systems. We enjoy the benefits of instant photographs and print-outs, pre-built homes, microwave ovens, and fast-foods.

These technological breakthroughs have brought us both benefits and burdens. On the one hand, they make many dimensions of our lives more flexible and more convenient. On the other hand, they frequently leave us with the expectation that we can transcend time and its limits in all areas of our lives.

That, as the saying goes, is the rub. We not only expect instant tuning on television and instant information through radio, we also expect instant skill and instant knowledge, instant wisdom and instant maturity. We approach relationships with the attitude that personal communication ought to be as rapid and as efficient as a weather satellite or a computer. We look for shortcuts to prayer and spiritual growth. We want God to respond on our terms and according to our schedule.

But there are some things that cannot be rushed. Good wine still needs to be aged. The rivers move at their own pace. The dawn cannot be hurried. The geese know when to fly. The salmon recognize when it is time to swim upstream. The bear knows when it is spring. The rose responds to the warmth of the sun. Despite our daydreams and our impatience, we cannot alter the slow unfolding of the seasons.

The reality of time also touches our lives in inward ways. As pilgrims and wayfarers we walk in time's current and we too must confront its limits. We can order a hamburger at a drive-through window, but we cannot learn to cook in five minutes. We can shoot Polaroid photos but we cannot capture the eyes of wonder.

It takes time to develop the skills of human living and even more time to deepen them into habits of the mind and heart. It takes long hours of intense training to become an Olympic athlete. It requires years of development and self-discipline to become an accomplished pianist or a jazz trumpeter. It is a lonely journey that transforms a gift into a practiced skill, and skill into art.

At the moment when the poet has finally discovered the words and the composer has found the music; at that hour when the dancer moves most freely and the painter gives final form to the colors—at that moment the long journey of time has found its season and creativity has discovered its hour. It is a moment of destiny when human vision expresses its uniqueness and praises the goodness of its creator.

I have sometimes thought that it would be a wise thing for everyone to plant a few trees and measure the growth of their lives by their continuity and persistence. It might help us to realize that the seasons of our lives cannot be manipulated and the pattern of our growth cannot be rushed. It might help us understand that not every story has a digest; not every interview has a verbatim; not every experience can be summarized. There are seasons of the heart that take time and careful tending.

It Takes Time to Believe

Like most other significant experiences in our lives, faith also takes time to grow. In our age we need to be reminded of this quiet growth of the Spirit. There is a tendency to place high expectations on religious experience today. It is often approached with the assumption that faith will bring immediate answers to our problems and instant comfort in the face of a confusing world.

We have come to expect that religion will make us feel better and that prayer will immediately take away the pain and the darkness. We too easily look to religion for instant transcendence.

Obviously there are some moments of intense feeling and emotion in our religious journey. There are times when we seem to be transformed by God's presence. But these are not necessarily frequent occurrences and they are experienced in a variety of ways. Some people encounter God deeply but quietly. Others experience the divine presence with intense emotions and a clear conversion of life.

For the most part, religious experience follows

the pattern of the rest of human life. It requires a quiet faithfulness to the commonplace, a daily response to the ordinary. It needs to be nurtured by the Word of God and strengthened by prayer. At times it must be affirmed and celebrated in community. It needs to be carried quietly and courageously into parts of ourselves that are still closed off by fear or selfishness. Faith grows quietly because, in the end, it is God's gift and it unfolds according to God's time.

On occasion it might be possible to use psychological techniques to induce emotional states or religious phenomena. But these are not necessarily signs of God's presence. We cannot force intimacy with God. We cannot manipulate the pattern or the level of religious experience.

Kerygma: The Proclamation of Good News

The early church was born in an upper room behind locked doors and terrified hearts. The Spirit of Jesus transformed these frightened hearts into courageous men and women of faith. The church was born in an energetic burst of emotion and enthusiasm. The Word went forth in the power of wind and fire: Jesus lives! Jesus is Lord!

This earliest proclamation of faith became known as the *kerygma*—the central announcement of salvation in Jesus and the call to repentance and conversion. The preaching of the *kerygma* was accompanied by a joyful intensity and an overflow of emotion. There were miraculous signs and the gift of tongues.

The disciples experienced the nearness and the

protection of the Lord everywhere they went. Many people were converted and the number of those who followed the "new way" increased daily. Everywhere the gospel was preached there was an experience of religious excitement and the expectation that the Lord would soon return in glory.

From Kerygma to Catechesis

But the Lord did not return immediately. The kingdom did not come in a final burst of glory. Instead, the life of the early church continued to develop. Throughout the Mediterranean world small communities of Christians continued to spring up. More missionaries went forth to preach the gospel. There were persecutions and difficult days.

Eventually the church recognized the need to go beyond the initial proclamation of the Good News in order to develop a way of growing in the faith. It had to develop some initial means of administering the growing communities of faith, of structuring various forms of worship, and of developing methods of continuing education. There was a clear need to help believers understand the implications of the *kerygma* so that it could touch their lives in depth. There was, in short, the need to develop Christianity as a way of life and a way of growing in the Spirit.

This more developed form of teaching became known as *catechesis.* The term comes from a Greek word which literally means to resound or to echo. It can be understood either as referring to the message itself as it goes forth into the world, or it can be interpreted in terms of the effect which the message has on the listener. In this case it refers to the way in which the believer hears the message "in depth" so that it resounds in his or her heart and echoes forth into life.

Catechesis was the early church's way of recognizing that faith is a long-distance run, a journey in stages, a way that encompasses one's whole life. Catechesis is the kerygma flowering into a mature way of living and praying. It is the good news lived in season and out of season, in the darkness of persecution or in the joyful times of peace and prosperity.

The Catechumenate: Model of Christian Growth

By the third century the church had developed a complete program of preparing converts for initiation into the community of faith. This program was based on the form of instruction or catechesis which had been developed in the apostolic church. Thus it was given the name of "catechumenate"—a structured time of prayer, doctrinal instruction, communal sharing, personal growth, and purification for those who wanted to enter the church as adult converts.

The catechumenate reflects the innate wisdom of the Christian way of life. It is the recognition that although conversion may at times be an intense and joyful experience, it is also an on-going call which demands to be nurtured and purified. The catechumenate is the recognition that commitment must be deepened by knowledge and shared prayer; that conversion and repentance are lifetime endeavors. It is the recognition that becoming a Christian is not a casual choice, and that remaining a Christian involves a sustained commitment to growth.

The catechumenate also reflects Christianity's respect for the freedom of prospective converts. It was the church's way of saying: take your time; come and live with us in prayer; prepare your hearts; weigh the options; test the waters of faith; know the demands of this way of life.

The church's attitude toward converts tried to echo Jesus' advice in the gospel of Luke: "Which of you, intending to build a tower, would not first sit down and work out the cost to see if he had enough to complete it? Otherwise, if he laid the foundation and then found himself unable to finish the work, the onlookers would all start making fun of him, saying, 'Here is a man who started to build and was unable to finish'" (Lk 14:28–30).

From the beginning, Christians experienced their way of life to be a gift from God which made radical demands on them. They knew that there would be moments of intense feeling and nearness to God, but they also recognized that there would be times of loneliness and struggle. They affirmed the need for building a vision slowly and for laying foundations of faith with loving care.

The catechumenate is the church's way of taking its time. The restoration of the ancient catechumenate in today's Rite of Christian Initiation for Adults comes at an important time in the church's work of renewal. It comes at a time when we have been trying to re-win the importance of evangelization and the central message of the Good News. It comes at a time when we have become more sensitive to conversion as a gift initiated by God and pursued in the freedom of the heart.

The Rite of Christian Initiation for Adults provides time for evangelization and for the various stages of the catechumenate as a preparation for the Easter sacraments and entry into the community. It includes time for instruction in doctrine, sharing in communal prayer, and service to the community. It celebrates the growth of the faith in stages. It recognizes levels of intensity and commitment.

The Rite of Christian Initiation for Adults reminds us that in the truest sense all Christians are life-long catechumens. We spend our lives trying to enter more deeply into the Christian mystery. We confront the ever-recurring call to conversion and repentance. We strive through prayer and worship to be purified and deepened in our response to the Word. We open ourselves to the Spirit so that our lives might resound with his voice and echo back in our lives the power and presence of God.

Quiet Growth: The Kingdom of the Father

The vision of faith as quiet growth is rooted in Jesus' way of describing the kingdom of his Father. When Jesus began his public ministry he issued a clear call to repentance. He called for a decision, a dramatic change of life. But he also balanced this call with a warning. He told his followers that they would have to take up their cross daily; that they must build their houses on rock; that discipleship is faithfulness for the long journey. The call is a moment, the journey a lifetime.

When Jesus speaks of the kingdom of his Father he does not use the language of theology or philosophy. He employs images from everyday life. He speaks the language of the farmer and the housewife. The kingdom of God is not an esoteric vision. It is not a dramatic emotional breakthrough that will transport us into another world.

The kingdom of God is a call to become sensitive to the mystery of life that is already around us. It is an epiphany of God in the ordinary—a shining through of the divine in kitchens, fields, and marketplaces. It is as down-to-earth as bread and salt. It is like seeds sown in the field, or a net cast into the sea. It is like the lamp that is lit in the evening twilight, or a pearl discovered along the seashore. It is as joyful as finding a lost coin or bringing home a stray sheep.

The underlying theme of Jesus' preaching is the call to become involved in a long-term commitment to growth. It is an invitation to let our illusions about life die so that the truth about ourselves and our future can begin to emerge.

We must be prepared to take up our cross daily, to travel simply, to pray without pretense, to forgive our enemies, to hope in the face of despair, to struggle against oppression, and to die without knowing all the answers. In short, the kingdom of God is like God taking his time in our life.

That Your Hidden Self May Grow

In one of his books, Jean Paul Sartre wrote that "by the time we are forty we have our face." This wry comment seems to suggest that by mid-life we have become the kind of person we are going to be for the rest of our lives. We can presume that Sartre is referring not only to our physical traits but also to our mental and emotional character—our values, our dreams, our outlook on life.

Is this really the case? Do we become so set in our ways by mid-life that we are incapable of further growth?

There is a growing body of literature today which clearly contradicts Sartre's point of view. Daniel Levinson, Gail Sheehy and other writers have explored the patterns of emotional development which continue to occur during and after we reach our middle years. Their findings suggest that the process of growth continues in significant ways throughout our entire lives.

The awareness of on-going growth has found fresh insight and expression in our time, but it is not a new idea. It is the theme which finds its roots in the Christian way of life. The possibility of personal transformation is the starting point of Paul's biblical spirituality. He knew from his own experience that one's inner self can literally be "turned around" in mid-life. He knew what it meant to be converted, changed, transformed by the grace of God.

This then is what I pray kneeling before the Father, from whom every family whether spiritual or natural

takes its name: Out of his infinite glory, may he give
you the power through his Spirit for your hidden self to
grow strong, so that Christ may live in your hearts
through faith, and then, planted in love and built on
love, you with all the saints have strength to grasp
the breadth and the length, the height and the depth;
until, knowing the love of Christ, which is beyond all
knowledge, you are filled with the utter fullness of God.
Ephesians 3:14-19

Paul's prayer on behalf of his fellow Christians at Ephesus flows from his conviction that there is a "hidden self"—a dimension of our inward lives that can emerge into being through the power of the Spirit and our own response of faith.

What is this hidden self? How do we come into touch with it?

The answer to these questions lies in our willingness to follow the way of faith. This journey demands that we open ourselves to God at ever deeper levels of our being. This is a dark and terrifying experience, and many turn aside from it out of fear or the refusal to risk the false security of the present moment.

There is a recurring temptation in human life to choose a static rather than a dynamic pattern of living. We too easily assume that we have grown as much as we are capable of growing. This temptation to stop risking further growth is all the stronger when we reach our middle years. By then we have made enough mistakes to be aware of our blindness and our moral limitations. We have also had some successes—enough to make us cherish the goals we have reached.

Out of this tapestry of failure and success, brokenness and integrity, we arrive at a self-portrait that feels vaguely secure, or at least adequate for what we expect from ourselves and the rest of our lives.

It is at this point that we face one of the most important decisions in our lives. Will we choose to stop growing and settle into a holding pattern for the rest of our days? Or will we follow the journey of faith and risk everything in order that our "hidden selves may grow strong?"

The Christian vision is clearly a call to choose the second option—the pathway to further growth. Faith is a stance of trust before God. It is our way of saying that God knows more about our deepest selves than we do. It is our way of letting go of our illusory forms of security and allowing God to reshape our hearts.

Our hidden self cannot emerge unless our external self—the false self of fear, the superficial self of pride—dies. "You must put aside your old self," Paul writes, "which gets corrupted by following illusory desires. Your mind must be renewed by a spiritual revolution, so that you can put on the new self that has been created in God's way, in the goodness and holiness of the truth" (Ep 4:22-24).

The hidden self is the self created by God. It is the self that has been expanded through prayer and renewed through trust. It is the self that has been stretched by pain and deepened by suffering. It is the self that emerges from the dark journey of faith into the warmth of God's love.

CHAPTER EIGHT

Walking Alone

"You will be scattered, each going his own way and leaving me alone. And yet I am not alone, because the Father is with me."

—John 16:32

YOU encounter it when you least expect it—at the end of a good day or after a gathering of friends; on Sunday evening or driving back from a day off; at a holiday party or in a crowded airline terminal.

You hear it in the night winds and feel it move in the morning mist. You see it in the snow-swept fields and watch it in the summer sun. You hear its sound in the distant call of a passing train or in the low rumble of a jet.

You recognize it in the eyes of others—your family, your friends, your fellow workers, the strangers you pass on the street. You hear it echo in you when a melody calls up some lost moment of nostalgia and the restless wonder stirs again.

It comes as a sudden letdown, a weariness without words, a yearning without form. It speaks out of life's illusions and painful encounters. It says that being secure is not enough. It reminds you of

the limits and fragile edges of all things. It says that there are seldom the right words and never enough words to say what is inside. It hints of a void and a lingering darkness.

You cover it well. You say that you are tired and that it has been a long day. You pass it off as the beginning of a cold or the end of a bout with the flu. You say that the children are irritable, that there are piles of work and too much pressure.

These are good reasons, but you know that you are only playing with excuses, toying with the symptoms so as not to disturb what lies beneath. Inside you recognize what is really happening. You know the feeling and the presence. You do not speak the words but you recognize the truth.

Without moving your lips, you name it in your heart. It is more than weariness, more than a cold, more than the pressure of work, more than depression. It is the restless search of your life. It is loneliness.

How Can You Live Such a Life?

A few years before I was ordained, a young law student asked me a question which I am still trying to answer. We had spent the afternoon doing volunteer work at Friendship House, an inner city community center in Washington, D.C. On the way back to the university, we stopped for a glass of beer. At one point in the conversation, my friend paused, looked at me quietly, and said: "Look, you know I respect your decision to become a priest. But there's one thing I don't understand. How can you choose to live such a lonely life? What's going to keep you going?''

Perhaps the reason I remember his question so vividly is that it was also my question. I had spent years wrestling with the same issue. It was not just popular opinion which linked loneliness with celibacy. Spiritual directors and retreat masters repeatedly underlined this aspect of ordained ministry. They challenged us to prepare well for a solitary life.

In the years since ordination there have been times of intense loneliness and search. There have also been deep friendships and the experience of community.

How can you choose to live such a lonely life? The question is still there. But the years of pastoral ministry and the close contact with people have given me a new perspective. It is not the question which has changed, it is to whom we address it. It is clear to me now that loneliness is not an experience which applies in some exclusive or special way to a celibate way of life.

Loneliness is not an issue which is related to this or that vocation. It is a question about the human condition itself. It applies to married men and women, to single people, to the separated, the divorced, the remarried, the young and the old, the affluent and the economically deprived. I have spent many hours with married couples who speak of a haunting loneliness in their lives. Sometimes I have heard this from couples whose relationships lacked some essential ingredient of healthy communication. But just as often I have

heard it from couples who, according to everyone's standards, had creative, loving relationships. Marriage is not a solution to the problem of
loneliness, nor is celibacy necessarily a more intense form of it. Loneliness is an experience that
comes with being human. It is part of the painful
beauty of being a pilgrim.

The Loneliness of a Long-Distance Christian

Placed in the context of Christian faith the experience of loneliness takes on a deeper meaning.
It becomes part of our call to journey with the
risen Lord. It is one more way in which we are invited daily to let go of the quest for security and
through the mystery of self-emptying love, to
discover our true identity in Christ.

We have been reflecting in these pages on various dimensions of the paschal mystery as it is
lived out in daily life. We have explored both the
darkness and the light of that journey as it is experienced in our common call to Christian discipleship. We have looked at Christian pilgrimage
from the perspective of running away, wandering,
turning around, setting out, following, and, in the
next chapter, will consider that of keeping on.

The confrontation with loneliness is related to
this latter dimension of the Christian journey.
The experience of loneliness is one of the ways in
which we are called to be faithful to the Christian
vision. It calls forth a willingness to keep on walking even when it is too dark to see or when we feel
abandoned or alone or simply filled with an overwhelming awareness of our failings and limitations. Loneliness becomes the testing ground of

the spirit. In this desert we wrestle with the questions of growth and the call to become whole. To live the paschal mystery deeply and fully requires nothing less than the willingness to become a long-distance Christian.

Levels of Loneliness

There is a common assumption that loneliness, like other forms or human suffering, is not healthy for human beings. Research tells us that it is possible to die from loneliness. The forgotten people in nursing homes, psychiatric hospitals, and prisons give strong support to this theory. Nevertheless, we must begin with the fact that loneliness is woven into the fabric of human experience. It is an emotion, a feeling. In its most primordial sense, therefore, loneliness is neither good nor bad, but simply a dimension of our lives. It comes laden with the ambiguity and fragility that accompanies all of the human condition.

How does this truth affect our attitude toward loneliness? It tells us that loneliness is not something to be done away with but something to be experienced. It is a threshold to cross, a pathway to walk. Loneliness will be a creative or destructive experience depending on how we approach it or walk through it.

Like hunger and thirst and other human emotions, loneliness reveals a need to be filled, a yearning to be satisfied. Some of our needs are simple. They can be met in a fairly direct fashion. If we are hungry, we eat. If we are thirsty, we drink. But it is not that simple with loneliness. Loneliness is more than a physical need. It is even more than a psychological need. It reveals something transcendent about each of us, something that the most effective forms of human communication cannot fully satisfy. For the sake of clarity we can speak of three levels of loneliness: physical, psychological, and metaphysical.

• *Physical Loneliness.* Sometimes after we have been alone for a long time it is just reassuring to be where there are other people. They may be people whom we know intimately—like our family or friends. They may be mere acquaintances—classmates, neighbors, or fellow workers. At times we can overcome our physical loneliness just by knowing that there are other people in the house or apartment building. On occasion it is enough for us to simply go for a walk along a beach where there are strangers or to stop for a sandwich at a neighborhood coffee shop. Physical loneliness is the longing to overcome actual physical separateness. It is not necessarily a desire for any more intimate communication than simply being in the physical proximity of other people.

• *Psychological Loneliness.* From our experience we know that it is possible to overcome our physical loneliness and still feel pyschologically alone. A crowded subway, a busy sidewalk, rush hour traffic—all of these can be examples of the "lonely crowd," that is, people who are physically close, but psychologically estranged. Psychological loneliness is the yearning to move beyond mere physical nearness to a sharing of inward experience and life through authentic communication.

It is the desire to be "discovered" by someone else, the radical need to be affirmed and loved unconditionally by another person. If this exchange of giving and receiving does not take place something within us dies. When it does take place we have discovered the mystery of love and friendship. Once we have experienced this gift, something irrevocable has happened. We will continue to know the mystery of loneliness, but we will measure it against the power of love. Friends carry the presence of their beloved in their hearts even though they may be separated by thousands of miles. Friendship is a bond which spans the miles and years with the gift of mutual presence. Love breaks the barriers of space.

• *Metaphysical Loneliness.* Going for a stroll in a crowded park can overcome our physical loneliness. Uniting ourselves in thought and prayer with a distant friend can overcome our psychological loneliness. But there is a radical separateness about our lives that no amount of proximity and no intensity of love can overcome. Even the best of friends cannot overcome this final space of the self. The ideal married couple will still experience moments of intense personal loneliness. This is not a reflection on their failure to communicate well or their unwillingness to share their lives deeply. Rather it reveals a transcendent mystery at the heart of our lives, an infinite longing for a final union, an infinite communion of life. This is a restlessness and a yearning, which, as St. Augustine has pointed out, can only be filled by God.

Aloneness and the Search for Self

What does metaphysical loneliness tell us about human life? What does it reveal about our attitudes and approach to loneliness in our daily lives?

There are no simple answers to these questions, but there are hints of what such an experience is capable of calling forth from us. We catch a glimpse of these possibilities whenever we confront the loneliness of our hearts. If we enter into the reality of our aloneness, instead of trying to fill it in with distractions or run from it in desperation, we may discover a deeper dimension of our lives. We will move beyond the experience of isolation to an underlying current of unity. We will discover that loneliness is not just a sense of being separate and alone. It is also a search to know where we fit in the stream of life and relationships that make up our experience. Loneliness is a cry. It says: I am. I exist. I matter. I am here. I make a difference. But the cry is open-ended and tentative. It is not only an assertion, it is also a question: How am I to be? How do I matter? Why am I here? What difference do I make? It is the realization that I am not yet who I am to become. It acknowledges at once that I am here and that I do not know exactly where I am going or how to relate to others. In this sense loneliness is like a searchlight that illumines the basic questions of our lives. It focuses our attention on what matters. It calls us to a depth. It confronts us with mystery.

When Moses encountered the divine presence in the burning bush, he asked to know God's name, and God said to Moses: "I Am Who I Am. This is what you must say to the sons of Israel: 'I Am has sent me to you'" (Ex. 3:14). Scripture scholars continue to debate the full meaning of this passage. But one thing is clear. Only Yahweh can fully and creatively say "I Am." Only God realizes the fullness of life that flows from complete self-identity.

As human creatures we speak our names and our identity as pilgrims. We say, "I am" without knowing the full implications of our words. We cry out "I am" in the night of our loneliness and wait in the silence for a response. We speak our identity through our work and our personal vision. We fill in the chasms and the unanswered questions by our creativity and self-expression. We speak the "I am" of our lives through our relationships. We listen for it in prayer and wait for it in solitude. We confront its limitations in sickness and suffering. Loneliness is part of the terrain of the Christian passover. Out of its deserts and valleys we learn to speak our identity. Out of its night we learn to speak the sound of our own name.

Loneliness and Solitude

Being alone and being lonely are not necessarily the same experience. One chooses solitude because it is an opportunity for personal reflection or a time to let life flow freely inside. One does not ordinarily choose to be lonely. Solitude usually refers to the experience of being apart from other people for awhile to think, to pray, to be silent. Loneliness comes upon us whether or not we choose it and whether or not we are alone. It is not limited to circumstances, nor is it under our control.

Solitude and loneliness are not the same thing, but they are related in important ways. Our human lives move in a rhythm of sleep and activity, tension and release. We need times of solitude and we need physical nearness. We can learn this basic truth by simply reflecting on the natural rhythms of our body—the regular beat of our pulse, the ebb and flow of our breathing.

When we avoid the opportunities for solitude we may well be running from the real questions of our lives. We may be trying to fill in the chasm of our loneliness with work or superficial relationships. To do so is to choose to live only on the surface. The result is not less loneliness, but a deeper sense of isolation, since the real issues of self and community have not been faced.

Solitude provides the space and time to discover that loneliness need not destroy us. Solitude is like the desert—it has its risks and terrors, but it also provides us with an open horizon in which we can discover the shape and direction of our personal journey. In solitude our loneliness can be transformed into growth and a deepened sensitivity to life.

Solitude and Community

Times of solitude are not times of private living in contrast to time together. The moments of solitude can be occasions when we discover a deeper sense of communion with those whom we love and care for. In his book, *Clowning in Rome*, Henri

Nouwen shares some insights into this bond between solitude and community. "In solitude," he writes, "we can come to the realization that we are not driven together but brought together. In solitude we come to know our fellow human beings not as partners who satisfy our deepest needs, but as brothers and sisters with whom we are called to give visibility to God's all-embracing love."

A creative experience of solitude can enable us to touch our inward life more sensitively and with greater understanding. When we encounter our uniqueness with greater clarity we also come to know that our abilities are gifts received from God and shared in the interdependence of human community. Solitude is the ground out of which authentic community arises. It is the energizing consciousness of friendship.

Mohandas Gandhi frequently reflected on the need for solitude in his life. He did not approach time alone as though it were an opportunity to escape from life's burdens. He experienced solitude as an occasion to discover the bonds which united him to other people. "I go apart for the sake of India," he writes in his *Autobiography*.

Gandhi's words echo the vision of Jesus as he offers his priestly prayer: "For their sake I consecrate myself so that they too may be consecrated in truth." The search to become whole on a human level and the response to the gift of holiness on a faith level are never private matters. Solitude offers us a pathway to community. Self-sacrifice is pursued so that it may be a source of consecrating others in the truth. Our lives move between the

ebb and flow of personal and community experience, but they are never really private. Only when
we choose to see ourselves as cut off and isolated
from others does loneliness become a destructive
experience.

The Solitude of Jesus

Jesus was not a loner. Even before he began
preaching the good news of the kingdom he invited others to join in his mission. Before Jesus
went to the crowds, he first began to form a community of disciples and friends.

Jesus was not a loner, but he knew the mystery
of loneliness. One cannot read the gospels without
noticing this quality of aloneness in Jesus' life.
We are familiar with the image of Jesus leaving
his companions and friends to seek out the wilderness where he could spend entire nights in prayer.
We remember the painful moments of loneliness
when Jesus felt himself abandoned by those he
needed most—the obstinacy of the religious
leaders and the crowds toward his preaching, the
agony in the garden, the desolation of the cross.

Even apart from these clearly stated moments
of loneliness, there still remains something
solitary about Jesus' life. He never held himself
aloof from the crowds or people. He spoke his
needs to other people with trust. He sought out
friends and celebrated with them. He begged his
disciples to stay awake with him. He asked the
Samaritan woman for a drink. He tried to find
grounds for reconciliation with the Pharisees. He

was available for the sick, the poor, the lonely and the outcasts.

All the same there is something solitary about Jesus' life. His zeal for the gospel, his experience of God, his understanding of human nature—all these set him apart. One senses a profound aloneness in Jesus even when he was in the midst of the crowds or seeking out a place of rest for his disciples. He reached out to touch lives with openness and vulnerability. He did not hold himself apart from those who needed him or those he needed. Nevertheless the profile of Jesus in the gospels is that of a solitary figure—alone all the more because he sought to create community and to teach the ways of love. Jesus is like the grain of wheat which had to go down into the earth alone and die in order to bring forth an entire sheaf of wheat. The loneliness of Jesus was the price he paid to create a communion of risen life. The harvest of his love is still being reaped in his body, the church.

I Am Not Alone

When Jesus joined his disciples in the upper room to celebrate his last meal with them, he understood clearly how dark the night was to become. He recognized the time of his loneliness. Ironically, it came at the moment when he most reached out to form community, when he gave his followers the sacrament of love and the gift of communion. Despite Peter's protestations of loyalty, despite the evening feast of solidarity, Jesus

could already taste the loneliness of the garden
and the abandonment of the cross. He saw his life
in the bread that he broke and the cup that he
passed—a life given, fragmented, shared, poured
out for the healing of others.

On the edge of night Jesus speaks of his aloneness. When the disciples insist that they now understand and believe, Jesus confronts them with
the bitter truth:

> *"Do you believe at last?*
> *Listen, the time will come—in fact, it has*
> *already come—*
> *when you will be scattered, each going his*
> *own way and leaving me alone."*
>
> (Jn 16:32)

Then Jesus utters one of the most striking
sentences in the gospel. At the very moment
when he faces his darkest hour of loneliness, he
says these words: "And yet I am not alone
because the Father is with me."

These words reveal the central relationship
which Jesus had with the Father. This sense of
communion was to stand the ultimate test of loneliness—the feeling of total desolation on the cross.
At the final moment of agony Jesus put into
words all the loneliness that has ever filled the
human heart: "My God, my God, why have you
abandoned me?" If these were Jesus' last words,
we would have reason to wonder whether or not
he really trusted what he had told his disciples the
night before. But they were not his final words.

Jesus' last words are these: "Abba, Father, into your hands I commend my spirit."

We ought not to miss the profound significance of this statement. At the moment of his death, Jesus broke through the last barrier of human isolation and yearning. The relationship of communion which he had with his Father overcame not only physical and psychological loneliness, but it also conquered metaphysical loneliness. At the core of Jesus' life there was an abiding presence of love. At the center of his existence he shared in the life of his Father.

There are implications in this for every Christian. The loneliness of Christ is often spoken of as though it were something which he endured. It is more than that—it is something which he entered into and passed through in order to arrive at a still deeper communion with the Father. In loneliness, Christ's journey becomes our journey. Christian life is not an attempt to escape from loneliness. It is a journey into and through loneliness toward communion. Because we share the gift of the Spirit as the center of our being, we also share the truth of Christ's risen life. There is a sense in which every Christian has already broken through metaphysical loneliness. We continue to know the darkness of loneliness and the experience at times of feeling abandoned. We do not always understand our feeble attempt to say "I am" or to reach out to communion with others. Nevertheless we can echo the truth of Jesus' words in our lives. We, too, can say: "I am not alone, because the Father is with me."

CHAPTER NINE

Keeping On

" 'Yahweh,' he said, 'I have had enough. Take my life. I am no better than my ancestors. Then Elijah lay down and went to sleep. But an angel touched him and said, 'Get up and eat . . . or the journey will be too long for you.' "

—I Kings 19:4-6

THE call came in the early afternoon. I was teaching fifth grade religion when the secretary appeared at the door, motioned me into the hall, and said, "There's an emergency in the hospital. They want a priest right away."

The medical complex was only two blocks away so I didn't bother with the car. I picked up the oil of the sick and hurried out the back door of the rectory. As I walked past the ambulance into the emergency room I could taste the dryness in my throat and feel the tension in my shoulders. An attendant motioned toward one of the receiving rooms.

"What's the situation?" I asked as I walked toward the door.

"We have a forty-five year old male here," he said. "Cardiac arrest. He collapsed on the as-

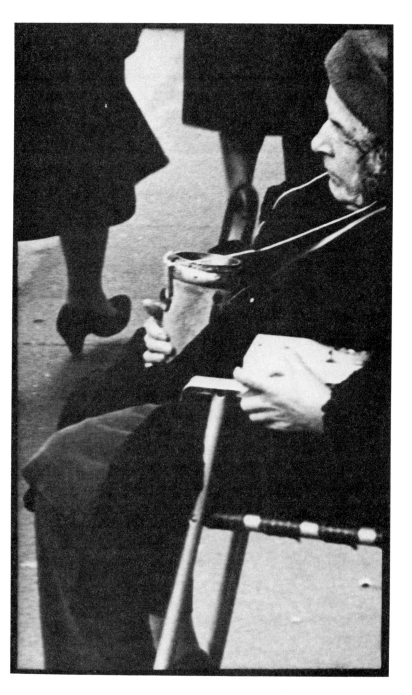

sembly line just after lunch break. Dead on arrival. They called his wife from the factory. She's on the way here now. She asked us to call a priest."

The next two hours remain in me with an emotional clarity that is startling. When the wife arrived, she still did not know that her husband was dead. As I broke the news to her she became hysterical with grief. Fighting my own feelings of flight, I alternately held her as she sobbed or stood by helplessly as she paced the room in shock.

It was not a time for words. It was not even a time for comfort. There was nothing I could do except be with her in silence and wait for the rest of the family to arrive.

The four children were scattered about the city. A twenty-two year old daughter was working at a department store. A nineteen year old son was in class at the technical institute. The two younger sons were in junior high school. They arrived separately over a span of about forty-five minutes. Each time the painful ritual was repeated: the initial shock and disbelief, the confusion and the anger, the sobs and the silence.

The reunion was intense and agonizing. I felt humbled and overwhelmed by the pain which the family shared with one another and with me. It seemed at times as though I were watching a slow-motion film of life. The gestures and facial expressions seemed elongated and final. The voices sounded muffled and distant.

But the pain and the loss were real. For an hour

and a half the members of the family clung to each other or lapsed into a dazed silence. It was not possible to run away from the reality of death. It was not possible to deny the pain. There were decisions that needed to be made. The doctors wanted to know if they preferred a post-mortem. The nurses' station inquired about funeral directors. The family mobilized their energy and dealt with the immediate decisions. At a certain point they knew that it was time to go home.

As they were leaving I asked the mother if there was anything I could do. She looked at me through tear-stained eyes. "There's nothing left to do," she said. "Nothing, except to face what has happened. There's nothing you can do. Nothing any of us can do. Ed is gone. He's not coming back."

She paused to let the full realization of what she had said settle inside. Then in a quiet voice, she said: "I guess there is something you can do . . . just pray that we can keep on going."

Keeping On

When life falls apart in front of us there is an understandable feeling that everything has ended. God has closed a doorway, cut off a road, ended a relationship. Suddenly there is no more reason for anything—no meaning, no light, no direction. Our energy is gone; our hope has disappeared. We are left feeling hollow and empty. What is there to live for? Why bother? Why keep on?

These are not rhetorical questions. They are

real issues of faith. We are like Elijah in the desert after fleeing for his life. We want to turn our faces into the night wind and let it be over. "It is enough Lord, let me die" (1 Kg 19:4).

"Just pray that we can keep on going. . . ." What strength was this bereaved widow asking for? Was she pleading for the courage to survive the funeral? The strength to keep from falling apart emotionally? All of this, but more. She was asking for the strength to keep on walking toward life instead of away from it. She was asking for the courage to let go without giving up, to surrender without abandoning herself to despair. She was seeking for a way to pick up the shattered pieces of her life and walk on.

In an emergency room we come face to face with issues of life and death. We confront the fragility of our lives and our relationships. We look directly at the apparent injustice of human experience, the unfinished business, the broken dreams, the stark fact of mortality. At times of crisis we are stretched to the limits of psychic endurance. We are forced to choose between hope and despair.

But we do not live our lives in an emergency room. We are not always confronted with crises. All the same, it is a mistake to presume that because a crisis is not immediate, the questions have disappeared. They have not. The questions that are raised in an emergency room are present every day. Keeping on is a daily task. It is the quiet challenge of the routine days of work, the lonely days of discouragement, the long nights of waiting, and the empty weeks of boredom. Keeping on has as much to do with today's laundry and tomorrow's groceries as it does with emergency rooms and the sudden death of a loved one. Keeping on is simply another way of saying that we must live each day richly and deeply.

Faithfulness to the Way

What keeps us going during times of doubt? What makes us long-distance Christians instead of curious bystanders? What sustains us when we lose our job, get a poor evaluation, encounter criticism, or grow weary of the struggle? Why do we keep on?

The biblical word for keeping on is "faithfulness." It refers to an inner quality of the heart, an authenticity of life that sustains us over the long haul. Faithfulness is not something we are born with or grow up with. It is not a characteristic that we can develop or build like we might build strong muscles or good lungs.

Faithfulness is ultimately a gift from God. We can learn to control our temper or to strengthen our will power, but only God can make us faithful. To be faithful is to persevere, not in blind tenacity, but with the full freedom of the heart. In Latin, *perseverare* literally means "to cut through" or to "continue on."

The faithful person is the one who cuts through the periphery of life towards the center, one who keeps on in the face of overwhelming odds. To persevere means that we not only follow a vision, but that we "follow through" to the end.

Faithfulness is not a blind sense of duty. It

does not mean that we have become rigid in the face of change or that we are as consistent as a machine. Faithfulness is deeper than consistency. It is a free, clear-eyed acceptance of the present as the pathway to the future.

Faithfulness is the way we keep our promises, not just those specific commitments to people and to tasks, but *the* promise to our deepest self and our creativity.

The Fidelity of God

In the writings of Paul those who follow the Lord are frequently referred to as "the faithful." We are given this title not because we deserve it or because we have earned it. We are called faithful because our lives have been touched by the risen Lord and signed with his promise. Our fidelity is rooted in God's faithfulness.

In Hebrew the word for faithfulness is *'emet*. It is a major quality of God's being, an overflow of God's seeking love. Yahweh seeks out a people and enters into relationship with them. This relationship is expressed in a covenant—a formal bond of mutual trust. *'Emet* is the word for the way in which God keeps the covenant. It implies an unswerving commitment to carry out his promise. "Know that Yahweh your God is God indeed," proclaims the author of Deuteronomy, "the faithful God who is true to his covenant and his graciousness for a thousand generations toward those who love him and keep his commandments" (Dt 7:7-9).

The distinctive quality of God's faithfulness is

that it is not dependent on our response. God is faithful even if we are not. He keeps on even when we give up. He is steadfast even when we are wavering.

Small wonder then that the Israelites referred to Yahweh as "the Rock." They found in him their security, their safety, and the constancy of knowing that he would always be their God. His promise will never be broken (Tb 13:14). His word will not pass away (Is 40:8). His plan is carried out to completion (Is 25:1; 55:11). Despite our changing moods and wandering ways, God carries forth his promise of salvation.

Jesus: Faithful Servant

Jesus is the enfleshment of God's faithful love. He is the promise come true, the new covenant, the final expression of the Father's love. In contrast to the Hebrews who turned against God in the desert, Jesus remains faithful in the midst of temptation. Unlike the religious leaders of Israel who care not for the flock, Jesus is the good shepherd, the suffering servant, the faithful prophet.

In the book of Revelation Jesus is referred to as "the Amen, the faithful one, the true witness" (Rv 3:14). And when Paul writes to Timothy he quotes from an early Christian hymn which celebrates the fidelity of the risen Lord:

> "We may be unfaithful, but he is
> always faithful,
> for he cannot disown his own self"
> (II Tm 2:13).

Jesus is the source of our faithfulness. He is the promise of strength that enables us to keep on walking. "Come to me all you who are weary and find life burdensome, and I will give you rest. Take my yoke upon you. Learn from me for I am meek and humble of heart" (Mt 11:28-29).

The Demands of Faithfulness

"Where shall we find a faithful man?" (Pr 20:6). This question in the Book of Proverbs suggests that fidelity is not easily achieved in human experience. One must search a long time to find one who is reliable in the Lord's way.

It is not difficult to be industrious or hardworking. It is not unusual to be successful in the market place. It is not unlikely that one could achieve fame in the world's eyes. But it is difficult to become a faithful person. Fidelity demands of us a radical honesty and an openness to God. It asks for a lasting commitment to a vision of life and a willingness to test that vision daily in our relationships and in our work.

If the call to fidelity was difficult to follow in the ancient world, it is all the more demanding in our age. A revolution of change and mobility has brought stress to all forms of personal commitment.

Our society does not place high value on lasting relationships. Convenience is more important than steadfastness. Expediency takes priority over meaning or value. It is difficult to be faithful in a world of throw-away commodities and temporary relationships. It is difficult to be faithful in a society which assumes that commitments are not made to last.

The statistics tell a grim story: One out of every three marriages fails. Friendships are tentative. Neighborhoods are in transition. We move frequently and make fewer lasting relationships. The pursuit of a career uproots us from our family and our friends. These are hard times for lovers, a recent popular song reminds us. The song simply puts into words what we feel in our depths. The times and the values of our society are not conducive to long-term commitments. We are bombarded with promises of the good life. We hear the call to follow the fresh breeze of freedom. It is easy, in such a setting, to forget that we cannot achieve a meaningful life apart from faithful commitments to other people.

Where Shall We Find a Faithful Person?

There are two characteristics of our culture which make it difficult to be faithful to a Christian vision of life. The first is the emphasis on self-fulfillment. The second is a pervading spirit of individualism.

There are historical reasons for these attitudes. The revolt against rigid social mores and role expectations has freed people to pursue their own goals and to create their own value systems. This obviously has its creative side. The search for fulfillment and the quest for personal identity has, in many instances, enhanced the quality of personal life. The problem is that these attitudes easily become goals in themselves. The result is often a sense of emptiness rather than fulfillment, and a feeling of alienation instead of identity.

There is a great deal written today about self-fulfillment. There is not much said about self-sacrifice or the value of relationships. Demanding one's rights and meeting one's needs is given priority over the responsibilities that we have toward society or the need we have to reach out to one another.

Despite the social movements and the change that swirls around us, there *are* people who are living faithful lives. Most of them are not making headlines or being recognized as outstanding personalities, but they are living the gospel and sharing its vision. They are husbands and wives who continue to wrestle with the unfinished work of communication in marriage; divorced people who pick up the broken pieces of their lives and begin anew; priests and religious who continue to give themselves to ministry under difficult circumstances; and there are elderly people who are living out their lives in hope and gentleness.

Faithfulness: Carrying Your Own Cross

When Jesus invites his disciples to follow him it is significant that he does not tell them to take up *his* cross. Instead he challenges them to take up their *own* cross every day and to follow him (Lk 9:23). We share the same human condition, but our gifts, our temperaments, and our circumstances are unique. Our cross is our life, our experience, our selfhood. It includes the unique events that we encounter in the journey of our lives.

We may feel at times that our cross is heavier than that of others, or that we were not given enough resources for the task of carrying it. We may think of our gifts as paltry, or our personalities as inadequate. We may feel that the circumstances and events that surround us are unfair or absurd. There are times when we might even feel abandoned and alone.

But St. Paul assures us that no one carries the cross of their life alone or without meaning. "The trials you have to bear," he tells the Corinthians, "are no more than people normally have. You can trust God not to let you be tried beyond your strength, and with any trial he will give you a way out of it and the strength to bear it" (I Cor 10:13).

Faithfulness as Letting Go

There is a profound difference between fighting against life and struggling on behalf of life. We are not necessarily faithful to life when we turn our faces grimly toward adversity or when we try to impose a rigid plan on the flow of life. As paradoxical as it might seem, "keeping on" also means knowing when to let go. "Lord, teach us to care and not to care," writes T. S. Eliot, "teach us to sit still."

Fidelity to a personal vision is not different from fidelity to the flow of life. We are faithful when we do not grasp at life as though it were something to be exploited. We are faithful when we are willing to surrender our wills instead of our values. We are growing in fidelity when we do not demand measurable results from our work and when we do not count on success as the only sign of personal worth.

Faithfulness is that quality of our freedom which enables us to affirm our value in God's eyes instead of measuring our significance by worldly standards. "You are not the oil," Hammarskjold reminds himself in *Markings,* "you are not the air—merely the point of combustion, the flash-point where the light is born. You are merely the lens in the beam. You can only receive, give and possess the light as the lens does."

This does not deny the necessity of personal effort. We cannot surrender to the creative center of life until we have struggled with it in the night and demanded, like Jacob, to know its name. We cannot let go of life until we have held it in our hands, welcomed it into our hearts, and made it part of our very being. When we finally surrender, it is with the knowledge that we have wrestled with the implications of our lives. We give ourselves to the flow of life with heightened awareness and freedom.

Our surrender is a victory, not a defeat. It is a triumph over our fears and our limited perspective. It is a break-through to freedom. Our letting go is actually a soaring leap into the center of living. At that moment we have become a faithful person—not because we have proven our worth, but because we have rooted ourselves in the fidelity of God.

Faithful in Little Things

When I was a young boy, I enjoyed sitting for hours and drawing pictures. One of the most exciting gifts my mother could bring home for me was a fresh pad of paper and a new pencil. Sitting down to a clean sheet of paper was an exhilarating experience, an adventure in imagination, an invitation to mystery. In a few hours I would fill up an entire tablet with pictures and stories.

When I would ask my mother for more paper she would remind me that there are two sides to every sheet and lots of room in between. But somehow it was not the same. There was something about a clean sheet that called forth excitement and wonder in me. It was like looking at a promise and knowing that it was yours to create.

Our lives are like fresh pads of paper. Each morning is like a clean sheet on which to sketch our lives. The days come to us one by one. They are ours to create, to shape, and to form the meaning of our existence. We can be content with a few strokes here or a hastily scribbled picture there. We can leave behind us a series of haphazard designs with no continuity or direction. We can even lose the sense of excitement that ought to come with a new morning and a new time to live.

Jesus told his disciples the following parable about what people do with their gifts and the time they are given to use them. As a certain master was about to leave on a journey, he summoned his servants and apportioned out his resources to them according to their abilities. To one he gave five talents, to another two, to a third one. "Trade till I come," he told them, and went on his way.

When the master returned, the first two servants had doubled their investment by using the gifts which he had given them. The master commended them for being faithful in small matters and promised to give them even greater responsibility.

The focus of the story, however, is on the third servant—the one who had received only one talent. "Sir," he said, "I have heard that you were a hard man, reaping where you have not sown and gathering where you have not scattered; so I was afraid, and I went off and hid your talent in the ground. Here it is; it was yours, you have it back." The master severely reprimanded the third servant because he had not used the gift which the master had given him.

The point of the story is simple and direct. God does not measure the value of our lives by the quantity of our productivity but by the quality of our hearts and our willingness to risk our gifts. We do not have to make a name for ourselves or leave a fortune for our children. It does not matter whether or not we have undertaken a project that will be named after us or changed the course of history. God only asks that we be faithful to the little things.

In the end it will not matter whether we have created a masterpiece or a simple design of love. The "what" of our lives will not count as much as the "how." The test of fidelity will be related to the quality of our daily response to the world around us.

How did we live our days? How did we use up the pad of paper? Were we faithful to the little things of life? Did we welcome each day with hope? Were we gentle with life and with people? These will be the real questions of fidelity.

Faithfulness to God is related to the fidelity we bring to an ordinary Monday morning or another day on the job. It is lived out in the care and the honesty with which we relate to one another. Faithfulness has calluses on its hands and a song in its heart.

CHAPTER TEN

Breaking Through

"There in their presence he was transfigured: his face shone like the sun and his clothes became as white as light..."

—Matthew 17:2

IN his novel, *Siddhartha*, Hermann Hesse describes the search for self-knowledge and spiritual enlightenment. Siddhartha, the son of a respected Brahmin family, is dissatisfied with the traditional life of his people. His restlessness leads him through a series of experiments with truth.

First, he leaves his family to become a wandering ascetic. In the forest he follows the way of self-discipline and meditation. He learns how to control his mind and to subdue his body. He studies the ancient writings and develops a reflective spirit.

As time passes, however, Siddhartha becomes disillusioned with this stark asceticism. Leaving the forest and the wandering band of monks, he turns toward worldly pursuits. He loses himself in the quest for sensual fulfillment and material success. He becomes a lover, a merchant, a dice player, a drinker, and a man of property.

After several years of enjoying the pleasures of the world, Siddhartha comes to realize that this life, too, has been shallow and empty. Nothing was capable of bringing him the peace that he sought. Nothing was able to quiet his restless heart. On the verge of despair, he arrived one day at the bank of a river. While he was waiting for the ferryman to arrive and take him to the other side, Siddhartha began to watch the river's flow and listen to its sounds. He had come to this stream before in his pilgrimage, but now, for the first time, he saw its beauty and heard its music. There was a mystery here that he had never before experienced.

As they were crossing the stream, Siddhartha shared his experience of the river with the ferryman and asked about its meaning.

"I have taken thousands of people across," the ferryman replied, "and to all of them my river has been nothing but a hindrance on their journey. They have traveled for money and business, to weddings and on pilgrimages; the river has been in their way and the ferryman was there to take them quickly across the obstacle. However, amongst the thousands there have been a few, four or five, to whom the river was not an obstacle. They have heard its voice and listened to it, and the river has become holy to them, as it has to me."

At the ferryman's invitation, Siddhartha decided to settle down next to the river. He too became a ferryman. He studied the sky and allowed the movement of the water to fill his life. He learned from the river. In its current he saw reflected the flow of his own life. In its sounds he heard the simple heartbeat of truth. That truth had been present all the while—within him and around him. But in the intensity of his search he had failed to notice it. He did not see the mystery in front of him because of his compelling desire to find truth elsewhere.

The Quest for Transcendence

The story of Siddhartha is not unlike our story. His pilgrimage is echoed in the experience of contemporary culture. Our search for meaning is akin to his in at least two important ways:

(1) We share a similar spirit of restlessness and a desire for self-knowledge.

(2) In our search for fulfillment, we often tend to look beyond ordinary human experience toward the dramatic or the unusual.

However confused we might appear to be regarding the value and direction of human life, there is no doubt that our culture thrives on self-reflection. We are a society of seekers. We are anxious to discover the truth about ourselves and about our lives. We are preoccupied with ourselves—our identity, our roles, and our feelings. Our restlessness is complicated by, or perhaps even occasioned by, the shallowness of contemporary culture. The priority given to success and the cult of personality often reduces one's identity to popularity and personal happiness to unlimited credit.

Even though we do not proclaim it, we are clearly dissatisfied with this superficial approach to meaning. We long for something more. We are anxious to go beyond the routines that suffocate us, the schedules that oppress us, and the tensions that surround us. We are serious about personal growth and self-knowledge.

Breaking Out: The Search for the Extraordinary

Where do we look for this personal growth? What form does the quest for self-knowledge take today?

The answers to these questions are as diverse as the people who seek for spiritual enlightenment. The search for fulfillment has many faces and forms. The shelves of bookstores are lined with self-help manuals and popular approaches to psychology. Various religious cults continue to promise instant security and salvation. Practically every year there is a new form of therapy, a new way of expanding consciousness, a new method of communication. Many people who have suffered from feelings of loneliness or alienation have found new hope through these experiments in self-awareness.

But these experiments also reveal the second way in which our quest parallels that of Siddhartha. Like the hero in Hesse's novel, we tend to look toward the unusual as the road toward truth. We assume that the meaning of our lives lies somewhere beyond the place in which we live and the time in which we journey. Not here. Not now.

We are like the pilgrims who come to the river and wait impatiently for the ferryman to take them across. In our search for transcendence we often fail to look at the flow of our immediate experience. It appears to us as something too ambiguous, too confused, too painful, too commonplace to carry the truth.

How can an ordinary day speak to us of God? How can there be promise in laundry rooms and vegetable gardens? Where is there truth in crying babies, alarm clocks, and the morning mail?

Our expectations often blind us to the mystery that surrounds us. We demand that fulfillment come to us with the proper labels. We want our parcel of fulfillment to be clearly marked and conveniently wrapped for easy opening. Our expectations about enlightenment deceive us into thinking that the truth about life lies in some esoteric experience beyond the limits of everyday life. We neglect the commonplace in favor of the ethereal. We stand before the river as though it were an obstacle. We want to break away from the ordinary. We want to break out of the condition we call human.

Breaking Through: Journey into the Commonplace

The Christian passage toward life moves in a different direction from the quest which we have just been describing. It does not look upon the human condition as a barrier to our search for salvation. It sees it instead as the sacred place where we encounter God and the meaning of our lives. In the paschal mystery we learn that the commonplace is holy ground. It is sacred because it has been embraced by God.

"And the Word was made flesh. . . ." These

words indicate the direction which God chose to walk in order to bring his love to us. We have heard these words so often that we easily miss their dramatic paradox. This phrase would have shocked the religious sensibilities of a believing Jew in the first century A.D. The Jewish religion emphasized the absolute transcendence of God. No image, no sound, no experience in human life could adequately reflect his glory.

In the Old Testament the Word of God is the expression of this divine transcendence. God's creative power is not dependent on the faltering words of human beings for its effectiveness. The Hebrews contrasted God's Word with "flesh"—a biblical term, which emphasizes the passing and limited nature of human life. Flesh shares the beauty and wonder of the earth. But it is also wounded and fragile. The contrast between Word and flesh is powerfully illustrated in this passage from Isaiah:

> A voice commands: "Cry!"
> and I answered, "What shall I cry?"
> —All flesh is grass
> and its beauty like the wild flowers. . .
> The grass withers, the flower fades,
> but the Word of our God remains forever.
> (Is 40:6,8)

The Word remains forever. The flesh withers and fades. What a paradox, then, to read these words in the gospel of John: "The Word became flesh!" The transcendent has become immanent. The God who had no name has become Emmanuel—God with us. This seeming contradiction is actually the mystery of divine love in the midst of human life.

The Christian quest for truth takes its direction from the pattern of God's journey. Our passing from death to new life unfolds in the form of an incarnation, an enfleshment, a plunging into the commonplace. The paschal mystery is not an attempt to break away from the ordinary. It is not a quest to break out of the human condition into an ethereal realm of truth. It is a breaking-in toward the depth of life. It is a breaking-through toward the sacredness of flesh which has been transformed by the touch of the Spirit.

Robert Frost describes the pattern of our journey in these lines:

> But God's own descent
> Into flesh was meant
> As a demonstration
> That the supreme merit
> Lay in risking spirit
> In substantiation.

Jesus is the builder of bridges between the human and divine. He *is* the bridge—the bond between the Father and human hearts. Jesus is like the ferryman in Hesse's novel. He invites us to look with new eyes at the river of life and to listen with the heart to its call. "Happy are your eyes for they see," he tells us, "and happy are your ears for they hear." (Mt 13:16)

Hear the Word of the Lord. . . It speaks out of the scents of grass and stars at night. It speaks out of the gentle hand of evening. It says: The river is holy. The kingdom is within. The treasure is hidden in a field. The leaven rises in the dough. The light shines in darkness. The seed falls into the ground. The beyond is in our midst.

Am I a Mystic?

Few of us are at ease with the title of "saint." Even fewer, I imagine, are comfortable when others refer to us as "mystics." All the same, St. Paul did not hesitate to address his fellow Christians at Corinth, Rome, Ephesus, and Galatia as saints. Nor did he hesitate to speak of the newly baptized members of the community as the "enlightened ones"—a term in the ancient world for what we today would call a mystic.

Why have we become so uneasy with these simple ways of describing Christian disciples? How did we lose touch with the roots of Christian mysticism?

It has something to do with forgetting the fisherman in Peter, the tax collector in Matthew, the Pharisee in Paul, and the carpenter in Jesus. It has something to do with forgetting the humanity in each of us. We turn saints into marble statues because we are more comfortable when they stand on pedestals. We transform mystics into bizarre personalities who engage in revelations, clairvoyance, and the occult, because at such a distance they no longer challenge us to see God in the midst of life.

Am I a saint? It is the call I received at Baptism, the gift I have been given. Am I a mystic? It is the daily challenge of every believing Christian. Saints are people who have been made holy by the gracious gift of God's love in Jesus. Mystics are disciples who are willing to spend their lives dying and rising with the Lord. A saint is a loved sinner. A mystic is a perceptive pilgrim. A saint is one into whose life God has broken through. A mystic is a saint who, in turn, breaks through to the mystery of God in daily life.

Secrets to be Kept

There are historical reasons for the uneasiness which we experience in accepting the call to become Christian mystics. The etymology of mystery and mysticism is found in the Greek verb, *muo,* which means to shut or close the lips or eyes. In the ancient Greek religion the "mystery rites" were ceremonial ways of initiating candidates into an experience of knowledge which was considered to be above and beyond the human. One who had participated in such a rite was referred to as a *mystes,* that is, one whose eyes and lips were sealed in secrecy.

There are several different theories as to why the element of secrecy became so important in the mystery rites. But the overall effect was to separate religious experience from everyday life. Mystics were considered to be select individuals who had broken out of the world of time into eternity.

This other-worldly mentality had an impact on the history of Christian spirituality as well. Some of the mystics in the history of Christianity were strongly influenced by the Greek view of religious experience. There is an other-worldly emphasis in their writings, which often portrays Christianity as a way of escaping from the pain and drudgery of human life into an ethereal world of union with God. While this view might contain some elements of authentic spirituality, it misses the mark of authentic Christian mysticism.

Secrets to be Shared

The true roots of Christian mysticism are not to be found in Greek religion but in the person and teaching of Jesus. He did not bring his message to a religious elite. He proclaimed the kingdom of his Father to the "little ones"—the outcasts, the poor, the sick, the forgotten, the searching crowds that followed him.

The gospel is not a theological treatise or an esoteric experience. It is an invitation to personal conversion. It is a call to union with God in the everyday through a communion of love with our brothers and sisters. Jesus did not give lectures; he spoke in parables. He told stories. He used the language and images of people who were close to the earth and in touch with their humanity. The gospel is at home in the sunny world of salt and bread, nets and coins, sowing and harvesting, living and dying.

Jesus challenges us to see the mystery of the kingdom as it unfolds in the ordinary. We break through to the kingdom when we become childlike before God and before life. We break through to the truth when we recognize that the river is holy and the morning is gift.

Christianity is a secret that is not meant to be kept. It is a vision to be shared, a mystery to be lived. "I became the servant of the church," St. Paul writes, "when God made me responsible for delivering God's message to you, the message which was a secret hidden for generations and centuries and has now been revealed to his saints. It was God's purpose to reveal it to them and to show all the rich glory of this mystery to the pagans. The mystery is Christ among you, your hope of glory" (Col 1:25-26).

The God of My Life, the God of My Work

Is it possible to live a life of union with God in the midst of a busy schedule? Can I experience God in the marketplace? The history of Christian spirituality answers these questions in the affirmative. The challenge of finding this "mysticism in action" is all the more important in our world of crowded schedules and psychic stress.

Some men and women in the church's history found it necessary to go into the desert or to a monastic setting in order to nurture the life of the Spirit within them. The tradition of the "desert fathers" is still flourishing in the monastic communities and in the religious orders dedicated to contemplative prayer.

But there is another tradition of spirituality which understands the call to holiness and mystical union with God as an integral dimension of every Christian's life. This is the "mysticism in action" of St. Ignatius of Loyola. It is the commitment to prayer and service of Mother Teresa and her sisters in the slums of Calcutta. It is the poetic vision of Teilhard de Chardin who saw the "divine milieu" as a loving energy that penetrates to the heart of matter. It is what Julian of Norwich refers to as "the courtesy and homeliness of God"—the wonder of the divine in the simplicity of the everyday.

The Hindus speak of this awareness of God in the midst of life as *karma yoga*—the discovery of divine love through human commitment and service to others. "If I could persuade myself that I could find God in a Himalayan cave," writes Gandhi, "I would proceed there immediately. But I know I cannot find him apart from humanity."

Jesus shared this vision of love in action with his disciples at the Last Supper. After he had washed their feet, he took his place at the table and said to them: "Do you understand what I have done to you? You call me Master and Lord, and rightly; so I am. If I then, the Lord and Master, have washed your feet, you should wash each other's feet" (Jn 13:13-14).

In her book, *Practical Mysticism*, Evelyn Underhill gives this simple description of mysticism as a way of life: "Mysticism is the art of union with Reality. The mystic is a person who has attained that union with greater or lesser degree; or who aims at and believes in such attainment." This approach presents mysticism as a way of life for every Christian. It reminds us that the God of silence and solitude is the same as the God of action and community. The God of my life is also the God of my work.

Mountain Tops and Valleys

Human life unfolds in cycles and seasons. There are moments of exhilaration and times of routine, summers of certainty and autumns of doubt. We move through light and darkness, joy and sorrow, mountains and valleys.

The transfiguration took place on a mountain. It was literally a peak experience for Jesus, not only because it occurred in a high place, but because it was an intense moment of self-realization and awareness. Psychologists of religion have described this event as a mystical experience. It was a breakthrough into truth for Jesus, a glimpse of risen life, a shining through of the Spirit within him. For a few moments his inner life became transparent. He experienced a profound union with his Father and an intense awareness of his own identity.

Christians have long been drawn to the transfiguration event. It stands as a promise of what we too can become through the gift of the Spirit. Like Peter, something in us cries out: Lord, how good it is for us to be here. Let us set up three tents. . . Let us stay here. If it were possible we would stop the flow of our lives or the unfolding of the gospel story. But the mystery of the transfiguration encompasses more than the experience at the summit of the mountain. It also includes the fact that Jesus returned to the valley.

Jesus did not remain on the mountain top. He did not withdraw into an ethereal world as a means of escaping the suffering that awaited him.

He came back to the sick, the lame, and the possessed. He continued to walk the roads of Palestine. He preached to the crowds and moved with quiet intensity toward that hour when he would climb another mountain to die.

The pattern of Jesus' life tells us something important about the nature of Christian mysticism. It indicates that life in the valley is just as significant for salvation as the moments of glory at the summit.

In each of our lives there are moments of breaking-through when we want time to stop. It might be the experience of falling in love or the quiet brilliance of a sunset. We might experience the nearness of God when we hold our own child for the first time, or welcome a loved one home after a long absence. It can be something as simple as listening to a violin concerto playing on a phonograph while the autumn sunlight streams through the window and creates patterns of light in the room.

These are times of transfiguration for us. They are moments of heightened awareness and joy. We ought to welcome them but not cling to them. They are gifts from God and glimpses of promise. They are also invitations to walk back into the valley with renewed hope. They are a quiet challenge to look for God in the ordinary and to recognize the flame of his Spirit in the eyes of his people.

CHAPTER ELEVEN

Breaking Down

"Unless the grain of wheat falls into the ground and dies, it remains just a grain of wheat..."

—John 12:24

I RECENTLY spent a few days with some friends in the mountains. During my brief stay I became good friends with their two sons—Darin, eleven, and Jagon, six.

One evening as the air began to cool, we all decided to go for a hike and watch the sunset. I noticed that Jagon began the journey with great enthusiasm. He had already put in a full day at the lake so I marveled at this added burst of energy. He ran on ahead and called out to the chipmunks that were playing on the forest floor. He threw rocks into the streams and climbed over fallen trees.

As the evening wore on, however, Jagon's spirits began to lag. At first he simply grew quiet and walked with the group. Gradually he fell behind and began to ask the age-old question of young pilgrims: "How much farther, Dad?"

At one point Jagon stopped and sat down at

the side of the trail. There were big tears in his eyes. "Dad, my feet hurt," he said. His father picked him up and carried him on his shoulders for awhile.

As we began the last leg of our hike, Jagon was once again falling behind. I dropped back to join him. He grasped my hand tightly as we walked the final stretch toward the cabin.

"Well, Jagon," I asked, "what's the first thing you're going to do when you get home?"

He looked at me with large, weary eyes and said: "I think I'll just sit down and wait till the pain goes away!"

Breaking Down: The Dark Side of Life

Jagon's response brought a spontaneous smile to my face. Perhaps it was because I was a little weary myself. Mostly it was because his remark seemed to carry so much wisdom in a youthful heart.

The evening hike had provided Jagon with a simple experience of human limits. I smiled at myself in his remark. I recognized a lesson that we must learn again and again. Walks, like vacations, are usually better in the dreaming than in the doing. A hike enthusiastically begun is not always a journey easily finished. Along the way we discover that there are letdowns in life as well as breakthroughs. We walk the earth and encounter our limitations.

Some of these encounters with pain are beyond our control and beyond our person. They wait somewhere in the silent forces of nature. They

come as violent storms or earthquakes. They appear as devastating floods or unending droughts. Even on the clearest day the sun must set and darkness must have its time. The wind which fills the sails and creates a path through the sea can also destroy the same vessel against the rocks.

Some of our experiences of limits are within us. Our muscles ache after a long day. Our feet hurt. We get dust in our eyes. There are dreams that do not come true and relationships that do not last. There are promises that are not kept and covenants that are broken. Our hearts fail us. Our lungs collapse. Our eyes grow dim.

Some of the pain is inevitable and expected: growing up, leaving home, getting old, dying. Some of it is sudden and traumatic: an unexpected illness, a car accident, a broken marriage, losing our job.

Whatever the circumstances, the encounter with suffering is a reminder that our lives are limited and precarious. We are vulnerable to forces that we cannot control or even understand. "How easily things get broken," the young priest in Bernstein's *Mass* comments as he gazes at the sacred vessels which he has thrown to the floor in a moment of anguish.

Human life thrives with an apparent resilience and an energy that is awesome. But it also has a fragile side, an unknown dimension of darkness and terror. The hero has his tragic flaw. The heroine collapses in a moment of emotional crisis. The round table cracks. The peace does not last. Life breaks down. There are times when the only thing we can do is to sit down and wait until the pain goes away.

This is Going to Hurt a Little

I can remember the first time I went to the dentist. He was a tall, imposing man who spoke with a gentle, reassuring voice. "This is going to hurt a little," he told me, as he readied his instruments and brought the drill toward my gaping mouth. In the next few moments I discovered that he had actually been trying to tell me that it was going to hurt a whole lot.

We try our best to blunt the effect of pain in ourselves and in others. But no amount of fore-warning can take away its impact. Despite our good intentions and our consoling words there are some encounters in life that will continue to be very painful. There is no gentle introduction to the world of suffering.

Attitudes Toward Suffering

We cannot remove pain from human life, but we do have the capacity of deciding how we will approach it. "Everything can be taken from a man," writes Victor Frankl, "but one thing: the last of the human freedoms—the freedom to choose one's attitude in any given set of circumstances, to choose one's own way." The attitude with which we approach the dark side of human life will, for the most part, determine whether or not pain will be a futile experience of absurdity or a purifying encounter with meaning.

Many people are familiar with the research

which Dr. Elisabeth Kubler-Ross has conducted in regard to terminal patients and their loved ones as they confront the experience of death and dying. Dr. Kubler-Ross describes five emotional responses which tend to occur as we face the imminent prospect of death: denial, anger, bargaining, depression, acceptance.

In the years since this research was published these five stages have been used as a model to help people understand their response to other experiences of grieving and separation. They have helped us to understand some of the most basic attitudes which we take toward suffering in our daily lives.

I would like to reflect on four of these attitudes as a basis for understanding the development of the biblical theme of suffering.

Hear No Evil, See No Evil: The Denial of Pain

Many people try to deal with suffering by denying it. The instinctive fear of pain in themselves or in others compels them to close their eyes and ears to reality. They put their trust in the folksy proverb which says: Ignore it and it will go away.

Perhaps it will. More likely, it will not.

According to an ancient Buddhist legend, Gautama's affluent father did everything he could to shield his young son from the reality of suffering. Before allowing Gautama to go outside the palace walls, the father would send his servants ahead to clear the road of any people or creatures who were experiencing pain.

One day Gautama left the palace without telling his father or the servants. Along the road he encountered three experiences of human suffering: he saw a sick man, an old man, and a dead man.

Stunned by the stark presence of pain, Gautama struggled with the realization that he had been shielded from the dark side of human life. For a moment he had literally stared death in the face. He knew that it was no longer possible to hide from the truth. From that moment on, the question of suffering became part of his consciousness and his quest for enlightenment.

The prevailing attitude of our culture is not unlike that of Gautama's father. There appears to be an unspoken assumption that if we do not see the face of suffering or hear a cry of pain, these will cease to exist as problems for us.

The world of advertising usually portrays a world in which pain does not exist. If pain is acknowledged, it is done so only in the context that it can be easily avoided or quickly overcome.

Likewise, the daily experience of watching the evening news becomes a study in denial. On the one hand we are confronted with insoluble problems, personal violence, and global suffering. On the other hand, during the commercial breaks, we are presented with a world of pain relievers, tranquilizers, and cosmetics.

We are easily left with the impression that the news itself is an unreal world of events and people that are outside our ability to change and beyond our desire to accept. The real world becomes a montage of slender models, healthy hair, youthful athletes, and soaring promises of happiness.

But the media is not the only dimension in which our culture practices the art of denial. We also deny suffering in both our social programming and our social values. We continue to be more comfortable when the elderly are in nursing homes and the insane are in institutions. We prefer that the handicapped not be seen on the streets. We erect fences around our junk yards and bury our nuclear waste underground.

For a time, denial can appear to be an effective way of dealing with the reality of suffering. But this is only an illusion. At some point the suffering of others, no matter how well it is hidden, begins to touch each of us. And our pain reminds us that we walk a common road. In the end there is no one left to clear the road of sickness and death.

Do Not Go Gentle into that Night: Anger in the Face of Suffering

If our first response to suffering tends to be, "Not me!"—the denial of pain, then our second response is often, "Why me!"—anger at a reality which we cannot change.

We take our health for granted. We know in theory that some forms of illness are part of the rhythm of living and growing, but when they occur in us we are seldom prepared to face them. After the initial shock of feeling sick or finding ourselves in the hospital, there is often a spontaneous sense of anger. Why me? Why now? Why here?

Some of our anger is toward the blind forces of life which led to this particular experience of illness or suffering. Some of our resentment might be directed toward others—the nurse who walks past in the hallway, our family and close friends who are healthy and functioning as usual. We may even experience strong feelings of anger toward God—a desperate questioning of his love and a demand to know why he has brought this pain into our lives.

These various expressions of anger are not something for which we ought to feel guilty. They are normal responses to pain, spontaneous reactions to the darkness which has suddenly descended upon our lives. Faith may enable us to see suffering as a blessing in disguise, but our immediate human vision only encounters the pain. And it feels more like the real thing than a disguise. "Do not go gentle into that good night," writes Dylan Thomas on behalf of his dying father, "Rage, rage against the dying of the light."

From the biblical perspective there is no reason to assume that God does not accept our anger as readily as he accepts our praise. There is a long tradition of "complaint literature" in sacred scripture. "How much longer is the oppressor to blaspheme?" the psalmist asks God. "How long will the enemy insult your name? Why hold back your hand? Why keep your right hand hidden?" (Ps 74:10–11).

In his anguish and isolation Jeremiah cries out to Yahweh: "You have seduced me, and I have let myself be seduced; you have overpowered me. You were the stronger. I am a daily laughing-stock, everybody's butt" (Jr 20:7).

These are not isolated outbursts that were included in the sacred text by accident. The human authors of God's Word clearly saw these anguished moments as profound expressions of dependence and faith in God.

With Clenched Fists: Cling to the Hurt

We usually think of Christian detachment as the willingness to give up the attractive things of life—material possessions, youthful beauty, fine clothes—for the sake of God and his kingdom. But there are times when we choose to cling to the unattractive and painful dimensions of life with even more tenacity.

Henri Nouwen recounts the story of a woman who was brought into a psychiatric center for treatment. When she first arrived she was filled with rage. With clenched fists she struck out at everyone and everything around her. When the doctors tried to calm her down they found that she would not or could not relax her tight muscles. They also discovered that there was one small coin which she gripped in her fist. It was as though she would lose her very self along with the coin if she gave it up.

It is not difficult to see this woman's behavior reflected in lesser ways in our own daily response to life. In the face of suffering we often strike out at the people around us. Sometimes we flail at them with angry words. Sometimes we retaliate with cold silence. All the while we are clinging to our anger and our hurt as though it were a weapon to use against the world, our last defense against the injustice of life.

It is spiritually helpful for us to be able to recognize and name our feelings of anger. Such honest self-knowledge is a sign that we love life even as we struggle against it, that we trust God even as we question him.

Nevertheless, there are circumstances in which anger becomes destructive. It becomes a destructive force when we cling to it or refuse to move beyond it. Anger that is nursed or intensified over a long period of time can become a life-long resentment. Then it is no longer a purifying energy or a creative force. It is only a debilitating attitude of the heart.

With Open Hands: Accepting Pain

How can we move beyond the bitterness and the hate which sometimes invade our lives? How do we pass through the anger, the jealousy, the disappointment, the desire for revenge?

The answer to these questions has something to do with our willingness to become more open to God and more vulnerable to pain. It is related to the power of the Spirit at work in us—a power that can transform our clenched fists into open hands.

One of the most natural symbols of love is an open hand extended in welcome. It announces a spirit of openness. It speaks quietly of trust and receptivity. During the times that we are angry or seized with fear, the muscles in our bodies tighten up and our fists instinctively become clenched. When we dare to let go of our anger our hands relax and our palms spread out in a gesture of receiving. The outward symbol reflects an inward reality. When we surrender even one of our fears, our lives become more open to God.

When someone tries to live in this spirit of openness we say that he or she is vulnerable to life. To be vulnerable literally means to be capable of being wounded. As paradoxical as it sounds, we can only be healed of our bitterness if we are willing to open ourselves to the pain of life. The first step toward wholeness is the willingness to be wounded.

This attitude of openness toward pain emerged only gradually in the history of God's people. Like most of the other nations which surrounded them, the early Israelites followed an unwritten law of vengeance and retaliation. They tended to meet violence with more violence. The so-called law of talons (an eye for an eye and a tooth for a tooth) was actually a first step toward controlling this spirit of vengeance. The psalms contain several strong pleas to God that he destroy those who had harmed his chosen ones.

The experience of exile and the long years of suffering purified the consciousness of God's people. Those who continued to trust in the Lord when they suffered began to realize that God would not abandon them. When suffering was approached with a humble heart it brought even deeper faith and wisdom. One of the highest expressions of this spirit of trust is found in the Servant Songs of Isaiah. These poems describe a just man who opens his life to pain for the sake of others. The servant walks toward life with open hands. In doing so, he becomes a foreshadowing of Jesus' redemptive suffering and a model for all Christians.

The Suffering of a Just Man

On the hill of the Skull our human hearts found a way through suffering. God's answer to our cry of pain was not to take it away, but to come and take it upon himself.

The cross, as St. Paul reminds us, is an absurdity to those who look for rational explanations. It is a stumbling block for those who will not accept the fragile and broken nature of human existence. But for those who like Jesus, are willing to open their hands and lives to pain, it is the way to salvation. It is the pathway to new life.

Father, into your hands I commend my spirit. These words are the highest response of the human heart to the reality of pain. They do not arise out of a human vacuum. Jesus is a Jew. In one sense, his final words are a summation of his people's long struggle with the mystery of suffering.

If we were to study the thematic development of suffering in scripture we would find echoed there the same stages of emotional search which most of us experience in daily life. In the earlier expressions of wisdom literature, for instance, there is an almost naive attitude toward the mystery of evil.

The traditional wisdom proclaimed that the just man will flourish and the evil man will fail. "To observe the Law is to preserve yourself," proclaims one of the proverbs (Pv 19:16). On the other hand, "The man who sows injustice reaps trouble" (Pv 22:8).

This was an over-simplified view of life based on generations of practical advice. But it denied or ignored a fundamental dimension of reality—what about the just man who does not thrive? How do we account for the innocent who suffer and the evil ones who are successful?

These questions are raised in the writings of Qoheleth and especially in the Book of Job. They are questions that reflect the second stage in the Hebrew approach to suffering. Job rebels against the traditional answers to the problem of evil. He insists upon his innocence and demands, sometimes in anguish, sometimes in anger, to have an answer from God. But his only answer is a personal encounter with the Lord and the challenge to trust more deeply in his ways.

Trust in the Lord—this is the underlying attitude which brings Hebrew consciousness to the third level of meaning regarding suffering. The exiles and "the little ones," the prophets and the suffering servants taught the Israelite nation that the final answer to suffering lies beyond denial and beyond anger. It can only be discovered by totally entrusting one's life to Yahweh and by becoming open to pain.

During his life Jesus wrestled with the mystery of evil with the same intensity that his ancestors had. He gazed with anguish at the oppression of his people. He reached out in compassion to the sick and the infirm. He pleaded with his Father to take away his own cup of suffering. And he cried out in near-despair from the cross: "My God, my God, why have you abandoned me?"

Jesus was not a spiritual phantom. He was no stranger to the human condition. He knew its pain from the inside and wrestled with the dark enigma of suffering to the very end. Jesus' final words can only be understood if we see them as flowing from the full experience of human suffering and the quest to understand its meaning. They become, at that moment, not a declaration of surrender, but a proclamation of victory.

CHAPTER TWELVE

Facing Death

"Can you drink the cup that I must drink?"
—Mark 10:38

I WALKED leisurely toward the boarding gate. For a change there was time to spare. The terminal clock indicated a full hour before the flight would be called. I studied the faces of the other travelers and gazed out the floor-to-ceiling windows to watch the sun disappear behind the western hills. The March sky was aflame with color. Above the horizon the evening star was already blinking. We will be flying into a night of stars, I thought to myself.

Everything proceeded on schedule. The flight attendants greeted us with professional warmth and took our boarding passes. The passengers jockeyed for position and then settled into their seats. Some of them engaged in light conversation; others hid behind newspapers or stared out the window. A few tried to sleep.

As if on cue, the stewardess appeared to ask us if we wanted something to drink. Another attendant passed out newspapers and magazines. Af-

ter some initial static, the omnipresent music began to play. It was a routine flight.

For a few moments I withdrew into the world of silence to touch the wonder and weariness that moves like a river beneath the surface of life. I opened my eyes and studied my surroundings. The seat pocket in front of me contained a brightly colored brochure. It could have been a wine list or a sandwich menu. It had the glossy surface and contemporary design of an in-flight magazine. But it was none of these. On the front, in bold print, were these words: JUST IN CASE...

Just in case of *what*? Just in case I lose my return ticket or forget where I'm going? Just in case my drink runs low or I've already read this issue of *Time* magazine? Just in case I don't have a pillow or the cabin is stuffy? Just in case I've mislaid my traveler's checks or forgotten my carry-on luggage?

I knew, of course, that it was the airline's way of coming to grips with reality. Even before I opened it, I knew that the brochure would be describing more than flight schedules or creature comforts. I read it with a feeling of detachment. It contained detailed information on what to do in the event of a sudden loss of oxygen or some other emergency. As we began to taxi down the runway the stewardess shared the same information and pointed mechanically toward the emergency exits. Then she smiled and announced that refreshments would be served shortly after take-off.

The trip was smooth and uneventful. We flew under a canopy of stars and landed in another city where people live and dream and go about their work. I walked off the plane and took the escalator to the baggage claim area. The trip was over, but the journey was not ended.

Just in case. . . It was a conditional clause in a world of efficiency. It was a technological slip of the tongue, a manufacturer's comment on mortality, a brief recognition that there are limits and unknown factors, a passing admission that life is not completely under our control. The brochure was a reminder on glossy paper that even at 30,000 feet the earth still claims us as its own.

Facing Life, Facing Death

In her various studies, Elisabeth Kübler-Ross has pointed out that denial is the first stage in the human experience of facing suffering or death. What she describes as a phenomenon in individual patients and their families can also be seen on a broader scale in society.

Our language and symbols often are based on the assumption that pain and death can be ignored or at least packaged in a manner that disarms both and makes them less threatening. We have an ingenious way of dressing up disaster. We put frosting over the human condition.

On the evening news human tragedy and brokenness are sandwiched between ads for tranquilizers and beauty aids. The nuclear arms race and international unrest are placed in the context of consumer products. One has the feeling that death and violence become less problematic if they are seen in the framework of the good life. Yes, tragedies occur, but to someone else. There are disasters, but in another city. And they are brought to you tonight by Proctor and Gamble.

The cigarette manufacturers invite us to associate their products with attractive, self-reliant people who make mature decisions and live in the open country. It is only as a footnote to these images of freedom and natural beauty that a warning appears: Smoking may be hazardous to your health.

In our society death is seldom looked upon as an integral part of life. More often it is viewed as a conditional clause or a hidden footnote. It is a brochure in an airline seat pocket, an eventuality that is put on paper in order to comply with the rules of the Federal government.

Despite our creativity, however, the human condition continues to break into our lives. Mortality is the fine print of every experience. Death finds a trap door. The ground comes up to meet us.

When he was still a young man Leo Tolstoy reflected on his awareness of death. "I should like to live long, very long," he wrote, "and the thought of death fills me with a childlike, poetic alarm." At this stage in his life, Tolstoy had not yet explored the depths of his mortality. He was like Job before the time of testing or Abraham before his call from God. Later in his life Tolstoy faced death at a deeper level of experience. The childlikeness was gone. The poetic alarm turned to terror in the face of an inexplicable darkness. At that moment, in Tolstoy's words, "life stood still and grew sinister."

Although facing suffering and death is a fearful experience, it need not paralyze us. As Christians we are called neither to deny death nor to give in to despair. We are invited to enter into the mystery of suffering and death and to walk through it toward the promise of new life. The gospel understands dying as an essential dimension of living. If we open ourselves to this mystery in faith we will become free for eternal life.

For a Christian, therefore, suffering and death are not conditional clauses or chance occurrences which are outside the control of technology. They are not marginal events in the human journey. They are an integral part of our participation in the paschal mystery of Jesus.

There is a cleansing honesty about the season of passiontide. In the events of Holy Week we are brought face to face with our brokenness and our mortality. In the picture of the Man of Sorrows we break through the euphemisms and the illusions regarding human life.

Lent walks past the glossy paper and the rationalizations and puts ashes on our heads. Holy Week leads us deeper into the heart of the paradox of living and dying. There are no artificial additives here. No pain relievers. No substitute words. The cross is a declarative sentence about human life. It is a statement about suffering and death that opens the way toward new life.

The Wine of Life

Scripture does not speak of life and death in abstract terms. The Hebrews were an earthy people who looked to everyday experiences and images to express the mysteries and contradictions that surrounded their lives. From their sheep and goats they obtained wool, milk, and leather. From the plants of the earth God gave them

wine to make them cheerful,
oil to make them happy
and bread to make them strong. (Ps 104:15)

Wine, oil and bread. These were the staples that sustained the Israelites in their daily quest for a secure life. These basic substances also provided the symbols which the Hebrew imagination employed to describe the beauty and the pain of being alive.

Of these symbols, wine is one of the richest and most versatile. Wine captures the bright joys of life. It is sunshine and fresh air. It is growth and transformation. Wine is the harvest of the endless cycles of wind and water, earth and fire. In its bouquet there is the freshness of morning. In its deep color there are desert sunsets and flaming hearths. In its warmth there is the sound of families and friends gathered together in celebration.

It was an ancient oriental custom to pass the cup of fellowship at every meal as a sign of friendship and peace. In this sense wine is the symbol of all of God's best gifts to his people—the land, the blessing of children, the harvest, and the gladness of sharing life in community. The Hebrews pictured the messianic times as a great banquet at which God would share the cup of fellowship with all his people. It is a time when, in the words of

Joel, *the mountains will run with new wine (Jl 4:18).*

"My cup overflows," sings the psalmist in gratitude to Yahweh, *"Ah, how goodness and kindness pursue me, every day of my life; my home, the house of Yahweh, as long as I live" (Ps 23:6).*

Wine is also the symbol of the covenant between God and his people. It expresses both the gratuitous act of God's saving love and the celebration of that love in community. *What return can I make to Yahweh for all his goodness to me?* asks the Hebrew poet, *I will take the chalice of salvation and call upon the name of the Lord (Ps 116:12-13).*

The Dregs of Life

In the heart of every person there is a longing for justice, a desire to make sense out of life. We do not find it difficult to discover meaning in life when we are experiencing good days. When we are secure we find life acceptable and even enjoyable. When there is bread on our tables and health in our families we can toast the wine of life with glad hearts.

But what of the painful times? How can we make sense out of them? Why do the innocent suffer? Why do good people have to face personal loss and tragedy? Is there any meaning in the anguish of suffering or in the darkness of death?

These are the questions of Job. They are questions which are as timeless and as enduring as the pitiable figure who first voiced them. We encounter these questions in the faces of the terminally ill and in the eyes of the severely handicapped. We hear them in the weeping of a mother whose son has been killed in a car accident. We hear them echoed in our own search for meaning.

In his play, *J. B.*, Archibald MacLeish has written a contemporary counterpart to the ancient story of Job. The eternal questions of pain and evil, suffering and responsibility are raised again—the search for justice and the quest to understand the human dilemma unfolds in a modern setting. Toward the end of the play, Sarah, J. B.'s wife, brings back a twig of life which she found among the ashes and destruction in the town. Cradling the twig in her arms she says to J. B.:

> *You wanted justice, didn't you?*
> *There isn't any. There's the world...*
> *Cry for justice and the stars*
> *Will stare until your eyes sting. Weep,*
> *Enormous winds will thrash the water.*
> *Cry in sleep for your lost children,*
> *Snow will fall...*
>   *Snow will fall...*

The human heart demands justice. We long for an order that we can understand and control. From this perspective J. B.'s wife reveals a profound understanding of the human condition. There is no justice. There is only the world. There are only cosmic forces and the impersonal finger of fate.

Is there a vantage point beyond the human demand for justice? Is there a different way of understanding pain? What significance does the Word of God see in suffering and death?

Scripture celebrates the joys and riches of the earth, but it also faces the reality of suffering. In the Judeo-Christian tradition the cup is a symbol of sorrow as well as joy. Wine is cheerful, but it cannot prevent the night. It is a drink of fellowship, but it cannot redeem the loneliness of a broken life. The wine of gladness can turn sour. The cup of joy is easily transformed into the cup of wrath. The dregs of life become bitter to the taste.

In Job and Qoheleth, in Jeremiah and Habakkuk, in the psalms and in the prophets, the Hebrew tradition wrestled with the mystery of evil. The struggle was not carried out on the level of theoretical argument, but in the hearts and lives of people who believed in God even as they questioned him.

The Hebrew poets did not hide from the darkness. They did not turn aside from the difficult questions of their age. They took the issue of suffering beyond the realm of philosophic problems and experienced it as a mystery which enveloped their lives. They pointed toward a mystery beyond justice. They opened the way to the compassion of God.

When J.B. asks his wife why she left him, she replies: "I loved you. I couldn't help you any more. You wanted justice and there was none—only love."

In every age there are people who feel abandoned by God. In each of our lives there are moments when we feel cut off from hope and from love. If we were to question God regarding these dark hours, he would not respond in the language of human justice. He would not try to explain away evil.

If we were to ask God why he abandoned us, he might well echo the words of J.B.'s wife. He might say: I have not abandoned you. I love you. When you demand justice on your terms and according to the narrow limits of the human mind, I cannot help you. You want justice and there is none. There is only love.

Can You Drink the Cup?

Jesus is the Father's answer to our cry for meaning. He is the Father's Word spoken to a broken world. When there were no scales to determine the relationship between good and evil, when there were no answers to our questions, God sent his son to be our brother. Where there is no human justice, there is still God's seeking love.

Jesus is the sacrament of God's compassion. He is the healing power of love for the outcasts and the exiles, the sinners and the brokenhearted. In response to the problem of evil, God emptied himself. In reply to the eternal questions God sent a Man who loved life enough to embrace death.

Jesus was a Jew. He was born into a culture which celebrated life's joys and wrestled with its darkness. No other human being has entered into the human condition as totally and as deeply as did Jesus. No other person has embraced the paradox of joy and pain with such intensity. No other person has walked into the mystery of living and dying as generously as he did.

• • • • •

In the gospel portrait of Jesus we see a person who was keenly aware of the earth and its beauty. We hear of a Man who walked in the morning sunlight and prayed through the long desert nights. Unlike John the Baptist and his followers, Jesus celebrated the wine of life. *"John the Baptist comes, not eating bread, not drinking wine, and you say, 'He is possessed.' The Son of Man comes, eating and drinking, and you say, 'Look, a glutton and a drunkard, a friend of tax collectors and sinners'"* (Lk 7:33–34).

Jesus went to weddings and dinner parties. He reached out to people of all races and social classes. His first miracle was a gesture of hospitality to a newly married couple. In the spirit of love and festivity he changed water into wine. The prophecy of Joel comes true in Jesus. The hills and the hearts are flowing with new wine. The kingdom is coming. The banquet has begun. Jesus spoke of himself as the bridegroom and described his kingdom as a great supper where one day he would drink the cup of gladness with his friends (cf. Lk 22:17–18).

The disciples responded eagerly to Jesus' vision of the kingdom. They were earthy men who loved the sea and sunsets and the warmth of human fellowship. They were anxious to test the ancient promises which God had made to their ancestors. They followed this new Rabbi because he spoke with authority and confidence.

Like Jesus, the apostles had a passionate love for life and its beauty. But something was missing. The vision of the twelve focused on the kingdom as a way to achieve personal power and fulfillment. They were anxious to enter into the mystery of life, but they were unwilling to embrace its paradox. They sought power without pain. They wanted to drink the wine without tasting the dregs. Despite Jesus' insistence on the necessity of service and suffering, they continued to spin dreams of power and glory.

In the end Jesus walked the long road to Jerusalem alone. His disciples accompanied him, but their minds were preoccupied with political kingdoms and arguments about status and positions of leadership. "Allow us to sit one at your right hand and the other at your left in your glory." The request of the sons of Zebedee came as a surprise to no one. It was a demand that all of the disciples wanted to make of Jesus.

The response of Jesus takes the form of another question. It is a question that is intended for all who will ever follow him: *Can you drink the cup that I will drink?*

The disciples answer easily and impetuously. Only later will they discover the full implications of drinking the cup of the Lord.

Can you drink the cup that I will drink? It is not just a question. It is an invitation.

CHAPTER THIRTEEN

Coming Home

"I came from the Father and have come into the world.
Now I leave the world to go to the Father."
—John 16:28

THE sun was already sinking behind the hills as
we drove north along the river. We rode in silence
as though each of us knew, without saying it, that
we wanted this time for ourselves. I watched
wisps of fresh snow blowing across the highway
to form drifts at the side of the road. I studied the
dark branches of trees silhouetted against the
crimson sky. The lights of dusk began to appear—
the evening star on the horizon, the headlights of
an on-coming car, the warm glow of barn windows, and the colors of Christmas twinkling from
picture windows and rooftops.

I felt excitement and anticipation growing in
me. Only a few more miles, I thought to myself.
We are almost there.

I watched the familiar landmarks as they appeared in the growing darkness—the creek where
we went swimming, the snow-swept field where I
cultivated corn, the familiar hills beyond the

river. Then, as though it were a long-rehearsed dream, we were turning and climbing toward the driveway. There, in the early darkness of winter, I saw the house and the land I called my own. There was an Advent candle in the kitchen window and a Christmas tree in the front room. I could see the figure of my mother preparing supper. The barn lights glowed through frosty windows where my father and brothers were finishing the evening chores.

I climbed out of the car and breathed in the crisp night air. I had waited a long time to see this picture again. For a few moments I stood motionless and silent to allow the scene to flow through me. It was just as I had imagined it would be. Lights in the darkness. A supper table. Smiling faces. Winter's warmth. Journey's end.

It was Christmas. And I had come home.

Homecoming and the Human Heart

Perhaps I remember the above scene so vividly because it was my first homecoming after a semester away at school. At the time, I was only fourteen years old and a freshman in high school. I had been away from home before, but only for brief intervals—an overnight at a friend's house, a trip to the city to visit relatives, a few days of camping, a week with my grandfather during the summer. But this was more than an interval. This was the first stage of leaving home in search of my own life. Coming home for Christmas was already a return to roots.

Home is more than a place. Even when we are young and growing up it is more than a geographical location or a name on the map. Home is a feeling of belonging, an emotion that prevades our lives. It is a reality that cannot easily be put into words. We associate this place and these people with the familiar and the secure. We recognize these surroundings as the landmarks of our childhood and our growth.

The bend in the road, the houses on the block, the holiday smells in our kitchen, the laughter in our living room, the view from our backyard, the playground behind the school, the trees of our neighborhood, the comfortable feeling of being called by our own name—all of these make up the emotional tapestry which we call home.

You Can Always Go Back

The word home speaks to us of safety and acceptance. It conveys an atmosphere of security and warmth. "Home," writes Robert Frost, "is the place where, when you have to go there, they have to take you in. I should call it something you somehow haven't to deserve."

Like birth itself, home is an experience of gift. We do not earn it. We certainly cannot claim to deserve it. Home is a given—a place of safety in storm and darkness, the last refuge from fear, the sure center of acceptance. In this sense it is correct to say that we can always go home again. Home is that place and those people who will always take us in. Long after we have grown up and followed our own way, our home remains a symbol of security. We carry it as an inner reality, a memory of rootedness, an image of the human heart's search to find a resting place.

Home Is Where One Starts From

At first glance, home is usually associated with images of returning to the secure and the familiar. But there is another side to the experience of home—that of setting out or leave-taking.

There comes a time when we must leave our familiar surroundings and walk toward the unknown. This setting out involves more than a day or a week or a few months. It is the task of a lifetime.

Leaving home is not so much a single moment in time as it is an unfolding process. It is more of an inward decision than a simple change in our outward circumstances. It occurs when we realize that the time has come to leave these people and these surroundings to set out in search of our own future. This does not mean that we will not return home. We will come back with more feeling and nostalgia than we knew when we were there. But no matter how deep the feeling, it will not be the same.

Life calls us forward, not backwards. In the mysterious unfolding of our lives, we are continually called to leave the past behind us. Home is as much a place to begin as it is a place to which we return. "Home," writes T. S. Eliot, "is where one starts from."

From Paradise Lost to Kingdom Come

As we leave home to find a job, to get married, to pursue a career, or to follow a vocation, the experience of what we mean by home begins to change. It changes not only in terms of physical surroundings, but also in the way we begin to think about it. Our original home gradually becomes an idealized image, an emotion that pervades our memory. Our attention, in the meantime, is directed toward the task of making a home for ourselves in new surroundings with new people.

There is a deep human instinct to make our surroundings familiar and cozy. Each of us has our own idea of what looks and feels "homey." We have our special pictures and our favorite colors. We arrange our furniture in a distinctive way. We look for an easy chair to call our own.

In an age of high mobility our physical location may change often. As a result we are challenged to move into a still deeper experience of what home means to us. We begin to see it as something beyond our physical surroundings. We speak of home as though it were primarily an attitude of the soul or a way of sharing with others. We seek out people with whom we can feel "at home," and we invite them in turn to "make themselves at home" with us.

In the process of our human pilgrimage a significant shift of feeling takes place. We continue to look back to our roots with loving regard. At the same time, we begin to shift our attention toward the future of our dreams.

How can we understand this strange turn of the human heart? What do our silent moments of nostalgia tell us about the direction of our lives? How can we begin to comprehend the mysterious hunger of our days? Are we restless because we have lost something that will never come back? Or are we longing for something which we have not yet found—something which will fully satisfy our inward yearning?

Wordsworth refers to these feelings of lingering nostalgia as "intimations of immortality." In more simple terms, we might call them hints of eternity or glimpses of God. In one of his most striking sentences Augustine reminds us that our hearts are restless until they rest in God.

Perhaps the true experience of home, with all the emotion and meaning which that word carries, lies somewhere ahead of us. Perhaps it is not so much the paradise which was lost as it is the kingdom which is coming. Perhaps home is our destiny rather than our memory.

Death: Dead End or Doorway?

We have been exploring the hungers of the human heart. The significance which we attach to these stirrings of the spirit tells us something about our understanding of human life. But there is something that threatens our hungers, something which must be reckoned with at all costs. Whether we characterize our human restlessness as a nostalgia for the past or as a yearning for the future, we must eventually confront the reality of death.

The issue must be raised. The question must be asked. Is death the final destruction of our life and dreams? Does it annihilate our past and our future? Does death destroy both our memory and our yearning for fulfillment?

From the perspective of human experience we cannot deny the apparent finality of death. Everything that we identify as life-giving and life-nurturing appears to come to an end at that moment. The warmth of our bodies, the suppleness of our skin, the movement of our limbs, the inner gift of awareness, all give way to rigidity, silence and decay. To look into the face of a dead person is, from an external point of view, to see the end of life.

From earliest times, however, our dreams and hopes have projected life beyond death. It is as though the hungers of our hearts are too great to be contained by the limits of mortality. The experience of love cries out for continuity. The vision of beauty demands an eternal realization. The flow of freedom soars toward fulfillment. Something in us reaches out for a future that will not die. There must be more. . . .

For Christians the undying hunger of the spirit for more life is realized in Jesus and his journey through death to new life. His paschal journey transformed the dead end of human mortality into the doorway to eternal life. The preface of the funeral liturgy states this central truth of our faith with characteristic simplicity: "In him, who rose from the dead, our hope of resurrection dawned. The sadness of death gives way to the bright promise of immortality. Lord, for your faithful people life is changed, not ended."

Death as the Final Breakthrough

From the dawn of civilization there is evidence that human beings have been interested in life after death. With the rapid development of medical science in our century this interest has intensified. In certain instances patients who had been declared clinically dead have been resuscitated. In carefully documented interviews these patients have described their journey toward the threshold of death. In his book, *Life After Life*, Dr. Raymond Moody summarizes the data which he collected in these interviews.

There are some common elements in their accounts. All of the patients speak of a form of survival after "death." After the moments of greatest physical distress which we associate with the moment of death, the patients often report hearing themselves pronounced dead by their doctor. Then they describe the experience of moving very rapidly through a long tunnel.

After this they suddenly find themselves outside their own physical body, but near enough to their former physical environment to experience themselves as spectators. Then a rapid series of events takes place. Former friends and relatives come to greet them and encourage them. A "being of light" appears to support and comfort them. The "being" helps them evaluate the meaning of their lives through an instantaneous playback of the major events in their human journey.

Suddenly they find themselves approaching some sort of barrier or border, apparently representing the limit between earthly life and the next life. At this point the patients discover that they must go back to normal human consciousness. Even though they are overwhelmed by intense feelings of joy, peace, and love, they find that the time has not yet come for the final breakthrough into eternal life. Later on, the patients try to tell others about their experiences, but they discover that human words have become inadequate.

Are these accounts actual glimpses of life after life? Or are they merely the projections of human consciousness under physical and emotional stress?

We do not have the means to answer these questions in a definitive way. At worst these experiences may simply be psychic hallucinations. At best they are accurate descriptions of the stages that lead toward death, but not of death itself.

Nevertheless, the collective data does offer some experiential affirmation of the Christian vision of faith. The experience of these patients points, however distantly, to the victory which Jesus has accomplished through his death and resurrection. Jesus is the first born of many brothers and sisters. He has already crossed the threshold of death. He has broken through to eternal life.

If home is where one starts from, then death is the final starting point, the last outpost of the human adventure. Death is not just an event which happens to us; it is an experience in which we become the central participants. In the words of Ladislaus Boros, death "is the first completely personal act, the moment above all others for the awakening of consciousness, for freedom, for the encounter with God, for the final decision about our eternal destiny."

Death as Home-Coming

The sailor at sea scans the horizon in search of a safe harbor. The soldier in a foreign land counts the days until he can make his way back to those he loves. The commuter turns off the toll road at the familiar exit and drives toward a house in the suburbs. These daily experiences of coming home are images and stepping stones. They provide us with fleeting glimpses of the final passage to new life. Death is life's greatest home-coming.

In his last discourse this is precisely the image which Jesus used to describe his impending death. "I came from the Father and have come into the world," he tells his disciples, "and now I leave the world to go to the Father" (Jn 16:28). Jesus' entire life was centered on his relationship with his Father. He told his followers that his food was to do the Father's will. His prayer was for the coming of the kingdom. And his life was a journey toward the hour when his Father would glorify him. To die was to go home to the source of love.

Jesus also speaks of our death as home-coming. He invites us to approach death with confidence:

> Do not let your hearts be troubled.
> Trust in God still, and trust in me.
> There are many rooms in my Father's house;
> If there were not, I should have told you.
> I am going now to prepare a place for you,
> and after I have gone and prepared you a place,
> I shall return to take you with me;
> so that where I am
> you may be too.
>
> (Jn 14:1-3)

Our lives alternate between the desire to set out and the yearning to settle down. When we are working we dream of what retirement will be like. After we retire we often find ourselves filled with restlessness. We approach death with the same ambiguity. One part of us resists dying because of our fear of the unknown. Another part of us reaches out for the future. It longs to let go of life's struggle and find a place of rest and security.

In his book, *Toda Raba*, Nikos Kazantzakis speaks of the tension between resisting death and welcoming it. As part of his reflections he recounts an ancient Hindu fable:

"An Indian struggled for a long time against the current which was pushing his bark toward the cataract. When the great combatant finally understood that his every endeavor would be futile, he crossed his oars and began to sing:'Ah, may this song be my life. I do not hope any more, I do not fear any more, I am free.' "

Like the Indian in the Hindu fable we move inevitably toward the cataract of death. We want to cling desperately to life. We resist the forces which seem to move us toward destruction. But at the moment we cease to struggle and place ourselves in the care of the Father, we become truly free. We move toward death with the realization that we are going home to God.

A Lifetime to Be Born

In the renewed rite of Baptism for children, the infant is welcomed into the Christian community by a simple gesture. The celebrant traces the sign of the cross on the child's forehead and invites the parents, godparents and relatives to do the same. In this silent sharing of symbol there is a wealth of meaning. We begin our journey as Christians under the sign of the cross. We carry this sign in the same way we carry our lives—as pilgrims and wayfarers.

The cross is at once the mark of suffering and the badge of victory. It is the *sphragis*—the seal under which Christians pursue the human journey. What the community has traced on the child's forehead must, in turn, be traced out in that child's life.

Neither death nor resurrection are experiences that happen only at the end of our lives. They are the pattern of each day's pilgrimage. Each time we let go of the past to embrace the future we relive Christ's paschal journey in our own flesh.

Each time we allow our fears or our selfishness to die, we break through to new life.

Each time we open ourselves to the Spirit so that he can break down the walls of suspicion or bitterness, we come home more deeply to ourselves, to our brothers and sisters, and to God. "I die daily," St. Paul tells us. He might have added, "And daily I am raised up to new life."

To live the Christian life under the sign of the cross is to recognize the dying of Jesus and his rising as they are traced out in our lives and carved out in our hearts. In such a context, death will not be a new experience for us. Neither will resurrection.

From the moment that the cross was first traced on our foreheads we began to practice the Christian act of dying and rising. The moment of death is an expression of what we are called to experience in less dramatic form each day of our lives.

It is far too narrow to limit our birthday to the moment in which we emerged from our mother's womb. That was but one of many death/resurrections in our journey. If the Christian vision is saying anything, it is that we spend our lives being born. Perhaps the real womb is human life itself. The pilgrimages of our heart, the struggle to become whole and holy—what are these except a further gestation of the Spirit within us?

Our faltering human vision points to the last turning point of life and names it death. But Christianity has always seen further and deeper than that. In the Roman martyrology we find a list of the outstanding Christians—those in whom the cross that was traced became a cross that was lived. For each of these saints there is a designated *dies natalis*—a birthday, yet not a day of physical birth, but the day on which these men and women were born into everlasting life.

The world struggles with darkness and the earth groans in childbirth. The human heart journeys forward in "a state of painful tension." But in the darkness there is light and in the groaning there is laughter. The whole of creation is on tiptoe to see the children of God come into their own.